A Mum's Life:
Coping with mental ill-health and motherhood

By

Dr. Diana Skibniewski-Woods

A Mum's Life

Coping with mental ill-health and motherhood

Dr. Diana Skibniewski-Woods

ISBN: 978-1-914485-19-0

Published by:

Design Marque, Pembrokeshire

November, 2024

Printed in the UK by Design Marque

Cover design by Design Marque

First edition

Diana Skibnieweski-Woods

Diana trained as a nurse at the Royal London Hospital in Whitechapel and Great Ormond Street Hospital for Children. After completing training to be a health visitor in East London and practicing in Bethnal Green, she married and moved to Wales, continuing in health visiting practice in Pembrokeshire for the next thirty years. Diana has had a special interest in maternal and infant mental health and completed a BSc. and MSc. focussing on the mental health pathway. On retiring she took an opportunity to do a research PhD. with Swansea University to research how mothers who have experienced mental health difficulties cope. She has published several papers on maternal/infant mental health, and as a qualified Therapeutic Yoga teacher was involved as co-writer and editor of a therapeutic Yoga practice reference book.

Previous publications

Swasthya, Yoga and Yoga Chikitsa to attain Sukha Sthanam and our true potential (2023). Compiled and edited by Yogachayra Jnandev Giri, Dr Diana Skibniewski-Woods and Yogachariya Dr Ananda Balayogi Bhavanani. Design Marque: Llandissilio.

The women I love and admire for their strength and grace did not get that way because shit worked out.

They got that way because shit went wrong and they handled it.

They handled it a thousand different ways on a thousand different days, but they handled it.

Those women are my superheroes.

Elizabeth Gilbert

Foreword

The transition to motherhood can be one of the most complex times in a woman's life. It is a metamorphosis, with a new life coming into the world also bringing a new life and identity for the mother. Yet it is a time where the realities are often glossed over, with women told that this new role will bring them pure joy and meaning, ignoring that many women experience significant challenges at this time.

In reality, overwhelm, loss, loneliness and even regret can run alongside her changing role and identity as a mother – emotions that often come as a shock due to the secrecy around this change. Statistics tell us that up to one in five new mothers will experience perinatal illness, a figure that is likely underestimated due to stigma and fear that still exists around admitting that this time is not pure joy.

We are getting better at talking more openly about these realities, especially amongst new generations of mothers sharing their truths via platforms such as social media. Gone are the discussions focussing on being 'blessed' and instead conversations about physical and psychological realities and how we cope with these are laid bare. But we often still try to 'fix' this through talking therapies and medication, seeing it as a temporary response to change and new responsibility, reassuring mothers that it will ease as their baby grows.

But what about those mothers who enter motherhood with a history of mental health challenges? What messages do they get about how the additional pressures of caring for a new life will affect them? How will they manage if we already have labelled them through a lens of not being able to 'cope'? And how do we view them? As fragile? Vulnerable? Needing immeasurable support?

In a 'Mum's Life' Diana very clearly shows us that we reassure them that they will be able to cope, and more than that, thrive. Through interviews with twelve remarkable women, she delves into their stories of strength and resilience, and the tools they used to adapt to motherhood alongside mental illness. She delves into the journey women go through in becoming mothers, where they sacrifice their own needs to care for their newborn infants but come to realise the importance of being able to look after themselves and their own needs too.

The book gives an honest account of the challenges that women face in motherhood and mental ill-health but builds on experience and lived wisdom to tell stories full of resilience and adaptation, with lessons for others to learn around what is possible when faced with a life changing challenge such as motherhood. Instead of a lens of adversity and vulnerability, the women within this book offer reassurance to others about how they will manage and adapt just as they have through every challenge until now. They remind us how many already have the tools of resilience, honed precisely through their previous experiences of mental illness. They have learnt how to survive and to thrive, to identify who will help and to feel control over their mental health. The depth and breadth of their knowledge and experience about living life alongside the challenges of mental illness is something we can all learn from.

This is a book about survival, resilience, and strength and I hope that it brings greater understanding, reflection, and courage to all who read it.

Amy Brown

Professor of Public Health

Swansea University.

Table of Contents

Introduction

All parents have strengths.
Crittenden 2008.

A Mum's Life describes twelve women's stories of coping with motherhood and mental ill-health. Their stories of coping every day were gathered using one-to-one interviews. A total of eighteen interviews gathered over 150 000 words of data and these lived experiences of coping are presented here using the mother's own words. The premiss that '*all parents have strengths*' is the foundation of this book, the mothers are strong articulate women who are able to share their lived wisdom of coping with motherhood and mental ill-health. The mother's names have been changed to protect their identities and pseudonyms have been used so that we can understand their individual journeys.

The focus is on women's experience of survival, through the examination of their knowledge of their own survival strategies and the development of their individual coping mechanisms in relation to the experience of mental health difficulties and being a mother. The experience and knowledge of mothers who understand mental health difficulties is a perspective not heard often enough and is in some ways largely undocumented, marginalised and unheard.

Coping is defined as "managing or dealing with something successfully" (Oxford Essential English Dictionary, 2011, p.133), but has developed within our society and mental health care provision to include how we respond to stress and adversity. For this project it was important that the focus was on the things that support human health and well-being, rather than factors that cause disease.

The initial chapters in this book explore the concepts of motherhood, mental ill-health and coping, to place the mother's experience within our current understandings. The remaining chapters use the mother's own words and are arranged around the themes and ideas which were developed from the mother's experiences of everyday coping.

Chapter One

Motherhood, mental ill-health and coping

This book is about the complex journey that we take through motherhood and how we cope on a day-to-day basis. I was fortunate enough to be able to carry out research with mothers who had experience of mental ill-health and ask them about how they cope on a day-to-day basis. These mothers were brave, articulate women whose wisdom is written here. I hope that you can benefit from their experience and learned coping mechanisms that have helped them. The knowledge of mothers' who have experience of mental health difficulties contributes to our understanding of the needs of mothers and babies and increases our awareness of their strengths and abilities that help them to get through difficult times.

Becoming a mother

Becoming a mother involves a psychological and emotional journey that must be navigated by each individual woman. It is an experience which can be filled with extremes of emotion from elation to fear, pride to shame, exhilaration to exhaustion. Pregnancy for many women can blur the boundaries of self, the knowledge of who you are as a person. Women may have a sense of losing their individuality as they adjust to caring for the needs of a newborn child (Maushart, 1999). The emotional journey that we take through pregnancy is an important part of the preparation for the arrival of our new human, but for many reasons it can be difficult to be open about how we feel. Women may struggle to talk about any negative feelings due to worries that they will be judged by others or seen as a 'bad mother'.

Loneliness and physical isolation are recognised as a problem for some mothers, but Stadlen (2004) argues that the real problem is not being understood. Mothers may not identify when they are successful and doing a good job because our language lacks the ability to express what 'mothering' is within our cultural norms. A mother who has given up her morning shower and her lunch for her baby, when asked what she has done today will probably say 'nothing'; whereas in reality she has been devoting all her time and energy to mothering. How mothers comfort their infants is an extremely complex skill that involves high levels of emotional competence but appears be to be taken for granted in our society today.

Motherhood is a time that involves high levels of personal growth and development and how we parent our children may be the most important decision we ever make. However, many mothers may feel that they are just muddling through as they juggle work, home and motherhood with little time for themselves. A common complaint in our modern age is that as women, we are expected to work as if we have no family commitments and parent as if we have no work commitments. It is sometimes assumed that our modern education and employment opportunities mean that women technically can have it all, but it can come with a cost to women. Maushart (1999) argues that there is a 'mask' over motherhood that minimises the enormity of women's work; women can lose a sense of self in caring for the needs of others.

The enormity of women's work appears to be passively ignored and positively accepted historically, socially and psychologically within our society. The caring role that many women naturally fall into is often accepted unconsciously by women themselves, caring for children and then caring for elderly parents is part of being a woman? But it's not so much that individual women might not choose these things but the expectation that it is done without consideration of the consequences for women and what they might be required to sacrifice.

Simone de Beauvoir a feminist author writing in the 20th century (1949, 1997) calls pregnancy a fulfilment of a woman's "psychological destiny" (p.542). She goes on to describe in brutally honest terms the transition for women in pregnancy as she sees it-

> *But pregnancy is above all a drama that is acted out within the woman herself. She feels it as at once an enrichment and as an injury; the foetus is a part of her body, and it is a parasite that feeds on it, she possesses it, and she is possessed by it; it represents the future and carrying it, she feels herself vast as the world; but this very opulence annihilates her, she feels that she herself is no longer anything*
> (de Beauvoir, 1949,1997, p.554).

The level of honesty in this quote feels unusual, but many women experience these poles of emotion during pregnancy and childbirth. Some of the emotional experiences that we have during pregnancy and childbirth are dependent upon external factors such as the quality of the birth and social support and relationships. However, as another feminist author Germain Greer (1970, 2012) in *The Female Eunuch*, points out "childbearing was never intended by biology as a compensation for neglecting all other forms of fulfilment and achievement" (p.109). Interestingly though she does spend remarkably little time discussing the role of motherhood in women's lives, considering the enormity of the role for most women whether they choose to be mothers or not.

Betty Friedan in The Feminine Mystique (1963, 2010) emphasises that "occupation housewife…cannot provide adequate self-esteem, much less pave the way to a higher level of self-realisation" (p.254). The questions for modern mothers' satisfaction in the role of motherhood is possibly not understood at a level that would reflect the importance of the role and the transition to motherhood can feel ignored and socially invisible. Some modern feminists question why if we live in an age of equality are women still left holding the baby: Rebecca Asher in her book *Shattered* (2012) comments that her illusion of equality was completely shattered when she had a child and despite determined efforts to share the parenting role more equally, she became the foundation parent in all areas of childcare. While the UK has advanced the political agenda on statutory maternity leave, the gap between maternity leave and paternity leave has widened. Whereas some women may find giving birth the most empowering experience of a lifetime, many other women do not.

What do we know about motherhood and mental illness?

Mental illness is one of the most common disorders affecting people worldwide with neuropsychiatric disease accounting for 13% of the global burden of disease (Callaghan, 2015). The period that extends from pregnancy to the first year of the child's life is recognised as one of the most significant periods in a woman's life. There is an increased risk of mental ill-health in the first year following the birth of a baby with between 13%-20% of women suffer from psychological problems during this period (Monteiro, Fonseca, Pereira, Alves, & Canavarro, 2018). However, this excludes pre-existing severe mental illness including: bi-polar disorder; schizophrenia; obsessive-compulsive disorder; eating disorders; and personality disorders (Viveiros & Darling, 2018). In terms of post-partum depression, some estimates are that over 50% of women are undiagnosed or under diagnosed (Payne & Maguire, 2019).

Risk factors for post-natal illness include life events and mental health history-

Moderate to strong risk	Depression or anxiety during pregnancy, Past history of mental disorder, Life events, Lack of, or perceived lack of social support.
Moderate risk factors	Neuroticism, Relationship difficulties.
Low risk factors	Obstetric factors, Socio-economic status.

(Henshaw, Cox, & Barton, 2017, p.11).

Interestingly post-partum depression is not recognised as a unique diagnostic category in the *Diagnostic and Statistical Manual of Mental Disorders* (DSM-5); it is classified as a major depressive disorder with a "peri-partum onset", that is an onset in the period shortly before, during or immediately after giving birth (American Psychiatric Association, 2013, p.186). Diagnosis requires five or more of the following symptoms-

  [] Depressed mood
  [] Diminished interest in pleasurable activities
  [] Change in body weight
  [] Insomnia
  [] Psychomotor agitation or retardation
  [] Fatigue or loss of energy
  [] Feelings of worthlessness or excessive or inappropriate guilt
  [] Decreased ability to concentrate or recurrent thoughts of death or suicidal ideation

(Payne & Maguire, 2019).

Despite the increased contact for women with midwives, GP's and other health professionals during pregnancy, identification and treatment of mental health conditions are lower in pregnancy than in women who are not pregnant (Viveiros & Darling, 2018). There are barriers to effective health care which include things like long waiting lists, concerns around stigma and inconsistent screening practices. There may also be a normalization and acceptance of mental health concerns as symptoms of pregnancy such as feelings of emotional isolation and loneliness (Viveiros & Darling, 2018).

Stone, Kokanovic and Broom (2018) identified a theme of 'what is not allowed to be said', finding that women may not want to disclose the level of their depression to health professionals, as they may feel that they 'should' be feeling happy. Additionally, there can be a level of discomfort felt by women towards the form filling diagnostic practices which are perceived as intrusive and bureaucratic (Stone et al., 2018). Childbirth is a significant life event, which can at times be actually life threatening or feel unsafe in terms of physical and emotional experience. This is possibly unusual in our modern world and therefore has an impact on us that we may not expect or anticipate. In addition, women must make a transition from being a single person to being responsible for another life.

The psychological process of adjustment to motherhood is important because it involves the developing attachment relationship between mum and baby (Henshaw et al., 2017). Having mental health difficulties can be associated with having poorer maternal/ infant attachment and there is longstanding evidence that a baby's social and emotional development is affected by their attachment relationship (Leadson, Field, Burstow, & Lucas, 2013). This makes the transition to motherhood a critically important time for women and children where effective support and care are vitally important.

Additionally, parents who experience mental ill-health can be vulnerable to other stresses and strains including: stigma; insecurity in the parenting role; concern over how to explain illness to children; difficulties managing the demands of parenting and mental illness; fear of losing friendship with children and difficulties implementing boundaries and discipline (Shor, Kalivatz, Amir, Aldor, & Lipot, 2015). The '1001 Critical Days' report states that the time, which includes pregnancy and the first two years of an infant's life, is an incredible window of opportunity in which parents need to feel confident that they can raise their children within a loving and supportive environment (Leadson et al., 2013). What happens during this critical period can lay the foundations for future health for the child in terms of emotional wellbeing, resilience and adaptability.

What do we know about coping?

When we think about coping it can be hard to define. It is a complex psychological phenomenon, the Oxford Essential English Dictionary (2011, p.133) defines it as "managing or dealing with something successfully". However, it has developed as a concept to include how we think about and experience stress and adversity. It can also describe how we try to restore our sense of identity and integrity. Our feelings of self-mastery, our energy levels and sense of wholeness and consistency are all part of coping. Richard Lazarus (1999) who writes extensively on coping, very much links the concepts of stress, emotion and coping as three parts of a whole relationship.

Snyder & Dinoff (1999) find that coping is aimed at lessening the physical, emotional and psychological burden linked with stressful life events and the daily smaller challenges in life. We develop strategies to 'cope', which aim to reduce our psychological and emotional burden. Success is dependent upon how effective these strategies are in reducing our distress, and how much they contribute to our longterm well-being. Coping may not always be able to end our stress but can often help us manage it better, through developing our toleration and acceptance. Lazarus (1999) suggests that our coping potential arises from our belief, that we can act in a way that can reduce harm or threat and bring about a benefit to us.

Coping can be categorised in many ways, we may have adaptive coping which can be seen as forward looking, flexible, largely conscious and attentive to reality, or maladaptive coping that tends to be rigid in operation and unconscious, a distortion of reality that largely attends to issues in the past (Snyder & Dinoff, 1999). So coping can be a conscious process, within our awareness or an automatic response that is outside our awareness. However, coping can work well or not according to the person, the context, or the occasion and may well at times contain things that would not necessarily be included in the understanding of resilience, for example in substance misuse, alcoholism, or self-harm.

Emotion focused coping is described as when we focus on controlling our emotions to prevent being overwhelmed by them. We can do this through seeking emotional support, or by placing the problem in context, or putting a more hopeful outlook onto the problem (Snyder & Dinoff, 1999). Whereas problem focused coping might seek to find a solution to a particular difficulty, by controlling or changing something or by learning a new skill, by removing a barrier or generating an alternative solution (Snyder, 1999). In this way, coping can be passive or active. Baumeister, Faber and Wallace (1999) point out that passive coping may be equally as demanding on the person as active coping, as it demands active control of the self.

Both problem focused and emotion focused coping are often used together; for example when we try to calm ourselves down, take some deep breaths or have a cup of tea, to think more clearly about a solution to a specific problem. Our success depends on choosing the right coping response for the specific problem within an appropriate context. Most commonly, we are more likely to use emotion focused coping when we assess a situation as one in which nothing can be done to change things. In contrast, problem focused coping is more likely to be used when, our assessment is that conditions can be changed for the better (Lazarus and Folkman, 1984).

This brings us to the importance of how we assess the problem that we are encountering. When we assess a problem, we can look at it in terms of the threat it holds and at the same time we are considering what personal qualities that we may possess which can help the situation. An initial assessment is carried out to determine the level of risk and a secondary assessment examines what resources we have that are available for coping (Lazarus, 1966 in Snyder, 1999). In theory the greater the assessment of control, the lower the stress in the situation. However, this is not necessarily the case if an illusion of control leads to unrealistic expectations or conversely feelings of helplessness when there may be things that can be done to help the situation (Lazarus & Folkman, 1994). Coping is found to happen in cycles, involving a shifting back and forth between a coping approach and withdrawal to re-appraise the situation.

Lazarus (1966) used the idea of a stressor/coping fulcrum, a balancing scale where our stresses are only interpreted as too much for us when they exceed our existing coping strategies.

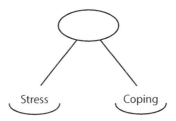

This balancing act of coping within our lives is always in flux, changing constantly according to our current stress and our current coping resources. We can however consciously build up our coping resources by taking positive steps for example, to make connections with people that are supportive to us, or by reducing our connections with unhelpful people, we can change how we approach a problem, or in some other way take care of ourselves.

This highlights the link between emotional intelligence and coping that has emotional regulation as the most important element. Without emotional regulation and the ability to remain calm or focussed in a crisis, we can struggle to perceive, appraise, express, analyse and understand the difficulties that we need to cope with (Salovey et al., 1999). Our personality traits also can influence our coping choices. For example, extraverts who are highly sociable can be more likely to turn to others for support, while conscientious people may be more cautious in their approach, and meticulous and organised people are more likely to engage in problem focused coping. Additionally people who are more negative emotionally, are more likely to be negative in their assessments and may suffer stress from their over-reactivity, whereas personality traits like stability and consistency can be more supportive to coping (Watson, David and Suls, 1999).

A crucial factor in successful coping does seem to be self-belief. Self-belief in our ability to overcome challenges and setbacks. Optimism is therefore an important character trait in coping. Our ability to thrive despite going through difficult times is linked to being optimistic and having creative character traits which can help us meet challenges. For example, having curiosity and imagination, or being emotionally responsive and open to new experiences are all helpful when we are building up our coping skills (Peterson & Moon, 1999). It may be that personality types who already experience a sense of personal control, are more likely to view emerging from difficult experiences as having gained valuable learning and understanding, and this can be a source of strength in the future (Peterson & Moon, 1999).

We also tend to develop characteristic defences that shape our personalities. Phrases such as, control freak, cold fish, hot head, drama queen, timid mouse, for example, may all indicate defences that form a person's personality (Burgo, 2012). These defence mechanisms can lead to coping by keeping painful emotions, thoughts, and fears outside of our awareness. The complexity and scope of these defence mechanisms is comment upon human intelligence and ingenuity and the basic survival instincts of human evolution. However having rigid or entrenched defences can prevent us from getting what we need and prevent us from accessing important emotions that we need to face.

The Ways of Coping Checklist, which comprises of seven scales is an interesting snapshot of coping, it includes-

- Problem focused- making a plan of action and following it
- Wishful thinking- wishing you could change the situation
- Growth- changing or growing as a person in a good way
- Minimise threat- making light of situation
- Seek social support- talking to others, accepting support
- Blamed self- taking responsibility for the situation
- Avoidant strategies- not believing in situation
- Help seeking strategies- seeking advice

Vitaliano et al. (1985)

24

The Ways of Coping Checklist places coping into descriptive units which are able to capture how people actually respond to stress when they contend with real life problems. When we consider how important coping is to our mental and emotional wellbeing, it is interesting that coping as a phenomenon may not to be measured as a routine strategy within mental health care today.

Another important aspect of coping is the consequences of the depletion of coping resources, leading to a need to replenish and recover (Baumeister et al., 1999). Recovery from stress and coping may require that the person finds a way to live that does not make serious demands on the self. A person may only return to feeling like their normal selves when they have recovered from the coping process and replenished the resources that were depleted (Rothbaum et al., 1982). The ways we find to cope are complex and infinitely variable, from person to person and situation to situation. Although people may have individual traits and characteristics, they cannot necessarily be predicted to react in a predictable way and even successful coping can be debilitating in its efforts to exert self-control.

Looking at resilience, coping and attachment

It can be the experiences of adversity that can prepare us to face future challenges. The term resilience is described as an individual's ability to be resistance to psychosocial risk experiences (Rutter, 1999). However, it is important to understand that protection from stress and adversity does not only lie in having positive experiences. Schore (2003a) finds that resilience in infancy is formed in the capacity of the child and parent to move from positive experiences to negative experiences and back to positive again, as the infant learns that negative states can be tolerated. In this way resilience is part of our early attachment relationships and an individual's central attachment relationship may crucially affect the ability of that person to be resilient.

In comparison with many other mammals, humans have a lengthy and vulnerable childhood, in which the infant relies on the care and protection of their parents, establishing the experience of dependency at the core of human experiences. If the needs of the vulnerable and helpless infant are not met by their care-giver, the infant will probably feel unsafe in the world from an early age and this will shape their ability to trust and depend on others (Burgo, 2012). When a child can internalise skilled transitions from positive to negative mental and emotional states and back again, they are able to respond resiliently in the future. The growth of the brain during infancy is formed by these early experiences, and healthy relationships function to allow us to think well of ourselves, trust others, regulate our emotions and maintain positive expectations about our lives (Cozolino, 2006).

Unfortunately, when our early experiences are fearful, it may lead us to being on high alert and hypersensitive to stress and this can be compromising to resiliency. Hyper vigilant alarm systems flood the brain with neurochemical and hormonal responses, which can over time impair the functioning of the limbic system and critically affect our ability to think clearly at times of stress (Karr-Morse & Wiley, 1997). Whilst having some stressful experiences may be important for our healthy development, resilience is more likely to be attained when an individual can avoid strong, frequent or prolonged stress (Herrman et al., 2011).

Our experiences are internalised into our body, this is known as somatic regulation and occurs through our vagal nervous system, which is part of the autonomic nervous system. When we face challenges, our sympathetic nervous system activates a fight, flight, freeze response. Depending on the quality of our attachment relationships, our vagal system regulates this sympathetic nervous system arousal and enables the cognitive and emotional processing that is necessary for maintaining healthy relationships. This helps us to be upset and angry without withdrawing and becoming aggressive with people we love (Cozolino, 2017).

Patricia Crittenden (2008) introduced The Dynamic Maturational Model (DMM) of attachment, which was developed out of the work by John Bowlby (1971, 1973, 1980, 1988) and Mary Ainsworth's work on the theory and models of attachment (Ainsworth, Blehar, Waters, & Wall, 1978; Ainsworth & Wittig, 1969). The DMM approach finds that as adults we use self-protective strategies which are developed from our attachment experiences in infancy, and we use these self-protective strategies across our life span. However, when there is an overreliance on past experiences within current contexts, our behaviour may be poorly adapted to our current situation. This is especially true when information understood in the past was missing, ambiguous or false. If our experiences have led to us having less tolerance for stress, change or challenge, this is known as having a lower vagal tone and can translate to being more impulsive, acting out, distractible and emotionally dysregulated. It also makes it more difficult for us to rest, recharge and recover from stressful experiences.

We can understand from this that our ability to form healthy relationships is dependent on our experience of relationships within our childhood. As adults, if we repress awareness of our need for other people, it may put us at risk of turning to other preferred substances, food, alcohol, drugs or other addictions instead, substituting them for the unreliable human contact (Burgo, 2012).

In this chapter we have looked at motherhood and some definitions and current understanding of mental illness within motherhood. We have tried to unpick what coping actually is, and lastly we have briefly looked at the relevance of resilience and attachment to how we cope as adults. Coping is recognisably complex. The term *coping* is used to describe how we understand an event as stressful, but also includes how we think we can cope with the coping abilities that we possess or can access. We develop strategies to cope across our life span and these are aimed at helping us cope with the stresses of life itself.

The next chapter begins to introduce direct quotations from the mothers themselves. These have been put into themes as the mothers begin to offer their insights into specific aspects of *coping* in terms of their mental health and being a mother. Some of their descriptions are poignant. They feel sad at times but are generous and offer us insight and understanding into the ways that they develop to cope. All the mothers who were interviewed were able to say that it was a positive experience for them to be able to talk about their experiences, and they expressed a desire to share their experience of *coping* with other mothers.

The mothers that were interviewed all had at least one child aged two or under at the time of the interview, their children's ages ranging from nine weeks to 11 years old. All the mothers' names and any identifying factors such as place names have been changed or omitted to protect their identities. However, giving the mothers pseudonyms was important as it enables their individual stories to be followed through the different themes that emerged from the interviews. A series of four dots in the quotations denotes when the mothers paused to collect their thoughts, whereas the occasional use of three dots denotes omission of some words in the text. The mothers came from across the UK, from Wales, England and Scotland, with one mother from Northern Ireland but living elsewhere.

The mothers described their mental health difficulties as ranging from: depression; pre-natal depression; post-natal depression; anxiety; post-traumatic stress disorder; bulimia; and obsessive-compulsive disorder. Some had co-existing conditions, and all reported that they had accessed health care in relation to their mental health difficulties.

Chapter Two

Mothers' lived experiences of coping

This chapter starts at the beginning by describing the mother's specific lived experiences of coping. The mothers were able to discuss and describe a wide range of coping strategies that they used regularly. In this first extract Ava, who has one child, describes using rationalising self-talk to help her cope with her child's behaviour. Self-talk can be defined as an internal position, where the person sending the message is also the one who receives it. Ava explains how she often reminds herself that her child's behaviour is normal and not something to worry about-

> *I still say it to myself sometimes now, yes he should know a little bit now but he's still a child, he doesn't understand and that's ok* (Ava).

Ava uses this reasoning to help her cope, it shows her ability to be reflective, and it is calming for her and supports her with regulating her emotions. Another mother Beth, who also has one child, similarly uses self-talk to help herself rationalize that the intensity of parenting is time limited, and this is helpful to her in terms of her motivation and her ability to manage-

> *I used to just repeat things to myself in my head, you know like 'it's not going to be forever'* (Beth).

Dawn who has one child, also uses self-talk to emphasise the time-limited nature of early parenting. In this extract Dawn uses repetition, accentuating the message that she is giving to herself, allowing it to stay in her mind-

I just keep telling myself it will get better, it will get better…. (Dawn).

In the next passage Chloe who has two children, shows her ability to think about things and motivate herself using self-talk. Chloe reminds herself beautifully that she must be doing ok by appreciating her children-

I kind of go I can't be that bad, this isn't who I am because look how I've done, you know and look how well I've done it because they're pretty cool (Chloe).

The use of self-talk features predominantly in the emotion-focused strategies with these mothers using rationalising self-encouragement to support their emotions. We all engage in self-talk, and the ability to have an internal conversation that is supportive to us, helps us to self-regulate. For example when someone tells themselves that they are 'doing a good job' this can be really helpful. Self-talk which may be critical or focused on negative aspects of situations can be less supportive and talking to yourself as you would a close friend is a more helpful perspective.

Hazel who has one child, identifies 'being organised' as a conscious coping strategy-

Although having a baby and being organised is kind of hard, they kind of don't go together really well, it makes me feel like I'm coping better, if I know if things are in order (Hazel).

Having this sense of mastery is enabling for her. She is able to plan and take effective action that makes her life more manageable. It is essentially problem solving in nature.

Beth also talks about her coping in terms of being organised and the ability to be organised is very important for her. She is clear that having a realistic approach for her is vitally important. She needs to be able to achieve something successfully, even if it's only a small thing. In this way she is not self-destructive by trying to do too much and possibly failing by then not being able to do it-

> *I think that being organised is one of the key things, but soft organisation, like being realistic about the amount of tasks that you can get done in one day, and you know, even if it's just one thing, like if you need to get the shopping, on any day of the week, plan that one day and make that your one task for the day* (Beth).

Faye who has a child under one, also mentions this 'realistic' element in her organisation and her expectations. She wants to feel that she has achieved something, even if it is only one thing. She can achieve something and have a sense of being able, rather that attempting many things and feeling a sense of failure with things being unachievable-

> *If I set myself a realistic expectation of doing one thing a day rather than getting overwhelmed thinking I've got to do this, this, this and that…. then I feel like I…. that really helps me mentally* (Faye).

Faye shows a development of this style of coping by recognising her responsibilities. In this longer quote Faye tells herself that things are time limited but also that they will get better. In a delightful way she looks forward to her child's happy interactions-

> *I have this responsibility now in life, um I have to get up and I have to go on, I have no choice um which sounds horrible but it's actually not it's a really nice choice.... um and also, I can tell myself this isn't going to last forever, you know something good and positive is coming around the corner whether it's her laughing at me tickling her belly or something, there's always going to be a positive with her* (Faye).

Faye is able to appreciate her interactions with her child and this helps her think more positively about the day ahead.

In this next exert Beth focuses on her ability to regulate her emotions. It is emotion focused and self-reliant in nature and emerges through a sense of self-discovery-

> *I kind of found a way to cope with it, by just walking away sometimes, just to go actually, I just need to go and sit in the bathroom for five minutes, like or even just 10 seconds to just breath.... and calm* (Beth).

Beth describes how she learnt to be able to comfort her child even in times of stress and exhaustion by calming her own emotional responses and regulating her emotional expression towards her child. This is protective for her child and demonstrates a parental protective capacity in her.

Chloe also talks about attempting to regulate her emotions but recognises that she finds it challenging. She uses the phrase "riding that wave", the wave of intense emotion, it is difficult for her to do-

> *On a really bad day it's about riding that wave and it does help eventually*

it's just that that wave is pretty horrible to ride. Um but I do find that the more that those coping mechanisms work the more good days I have (Chloe).

Chloe understands that when she is able to tolerate her emotional distress and allow herself to return to a state of calm without taking action out of her distress. This is effective in terms of her coping. The more she can do this the more effective she finds it as one of her coping mechanisms.

Ellie a mother of two children under three years old, describes being able to seek emotional support. She values the experience and understanding of someone that has been through a similar experience to her and she feels able to talk about things when she is having a bad day-

> *My sister, my sister is really good because she's done it all, she's been through counselling, she's been on medication, she's been off her medication now for three years, so she really gets it, so she's really good to talk to on a bad day* (Ellie).

Ellie deliberately seeks support from someone that she is confident will understand her situation. Perhaps talking to someone who had not the experiential understanding would be more difficult or less helpful to her, Ellie has no fear of judgment from her sister because her sister has experience and can therefore be a trusted source of emotional support and can assist Ellie in regulating her emotions.

Faye reminds herself that she chose to have a child. It is what she wanted, no matter how distressed she feels-

You know it's my choice, it's what I want to do (Faye).

This sense of taking responsibility for life choices is a type of acceptance and helps give meaning to the experience that she is having. It also makes her feel less powerless perhaps, as it is her own choice.

Beth finds strength from listening to her positive thoughts, but she has to pick them out from her more negative thoughts-

> *I just wanted to, to run away, but, there was all these things in the back of my head saying 'you can't do this', 'you can't do this', 'you've got to work on this bond because one day it will be worth it'. And it is worth it now, but at the time like it was absolute hell (laughs)* (Beth).

Beth here is expressing thoughts that were helpful to her in her struggle that came from another part of her being, a part that was able to encourage and motivate her. Her description of "absolute hell" leaves no doubt about the depth of her feelings at the time. Her laugh indicates the level of difficulty for her. It is possibly an acknowledgement of her pain, a recognition of the contrasting of "hell" and "worth it" in her account.

Chloe describes her coping strategy of saying things out loud-

> *To hear it out loud can actually make it really funny, because it's such a silly thing to worry about that's not going to happen* (Chloe).

Having a tiny, vulnerable baby to care for can raise all kinds of anxiety and fear for mothers, which are often protective in nature.

However when spoken out loud they may not all sound rational and this enables Chloe to emotionally regulate her fears. It is an example of self-directed emotional regulation. Chloe points out that she can see the funny side when she says it out loud, it does not sound like a realistic concern to her, but it feels like a sad form of laughter, a way of normalising her fears, convincing herself that things are actually ok. Her use of the word "silly" could imply that she feels foolish for having some of her fears, she is not confident in her own judgement. This is not positive in some ways, in that there is an element of self-denigration. However, in terms of re-negotiating her anxieties it is an effective coping strategy for her.

In terms of coping Grace who has two children, is able to identify many sources of resilience-

> *Probably in the most difficult times I would have got.... tried to hold it together until (husband) got home, and then quite often just gone out by myself, like on a walk or something like that and kind of tried to clear my head, umm quite often planned things that were going to help me* (Grace).

This coping includes some passive coping in the self-control and but then positive emotional coping in finding time for self and some space to think and restore. The rational thinking coping skill is also present on the holding on in the sense of time 'holding it together' in the awareness that it is time limited and that relief will be available at a later time.

Hazel also identifies that spending time outside is helpful to her. She is able to identify that being in the quiet of nature she is able to find a sense of balance-

Yes being outdoors, it always balances me so getting outdoors as much as possible is a coping strategy I think.... (Hazel).

When asked what is it about being outdoors that is so helpful? She answers-

Ahh.... the quiet I suppose, the fresh air, I'm not from a city, so I grew up in (place name) so I'm I would spend a lot of time outdoors I would spend a lot of time at the beach by the sea, in the woods, things like that, so um I think that kind of.... I think there is just something about being in nature I guess that kind of balances me. (Hazel).

In a similar way to Grace, Hazel is able to appreciate this as a coping strategy. This recognition of the effectiveness of a coping strategy enables it to be used purposefully to facilitate coping. The recognition of coping strategies also enables the development of a coping repertoire that can be consciously accessed in times of need.

Isla who has a baby under six months old talks of being in survival mode-

I think we were both just in survival mode (Isla).

This for some might indicate her not coping. However the managing of moment by moment, surviving each day may resonate with many parents in the early days of caring for a new-born infant. In a similar way to Isla's "survival mode", Jinny a mother of three, describes how at times she faced the world on what she describes as 'auto-pilot'-

That was obviously auto-pilot I was quite emotionless, because I got upset about a lot of things so I just turned my emotions off to the world, I would get up sort (children) out to go to school, send them to school, get ready for work, go to work (Jinny).

This is potentially mal-adaptive in style, but it is also protective in some ways. It is an escape, a mental withdrawal, a break from the distress and possibly a way to survive until things improve for her. Here Jinny relates a complex aspect of her coping-

When I have my GP reviews it's... yes never been suicidal thoughts it's always just that I can't cope, that I need to be able to want to cope (Jinny).

The needing to want to cope is hugely significant because without that what do you have? It is an aspect of her depression that is creating a difficulty with motivation for her. The way that she copes with this stagnant state is really inspiring. She describes being able to do something different that could break the stagnation-

That was the biggest thing to do something that was out of our routine (Jinny).

In terms of coping this is taking effective action. It is problem solving and strategizing. It did not have to be anything big, but just breaking the routine and shaking things up a bit-

I do like to be in control, and I like to have a set routine and when things are out of my control then I do feel that I can't cope, but I can't remember what the thinking was behind having that change in the routine then, it was mainly just to snap me out of my way of thinking (Jinny).

There is a high level of self-awareness here. Jinny recognises her need to be in control and stick to her prescribed routines. She also recognises that when this does not happen, she feels unable to cope. The likelihood of feeling out of control when caring for a new-born is possibly fairly high as the levels of need and manageability in caring for new-born babies are unpredictable. However, the changing up of the day's activities was really helpful for Jinny, enabling her to accommodate in a more flexible way the levels of difficulty that are present for her.

Kelly a mother of two children under four years old, describes using logical thinking when she is tipping in to catastrophizing thought patterns-

> *You tend to find like five things go wrong you know in a row and it's hard.... sometimes I will ring my mum then, in a bit of a tis and she tries to remind me that you know it's not necessarily.... like those five things aren't necessarily connected, they just happened to have happened together and you know it doesn't have to be a negative rest of the day just accept that they were all a bunch of bad co-incidences kind of thing* (Kelly).

Kelly is able to seek support from someone that she trusts and with her help is able to dispel the feeling that everything will go wrong because a few things have gone wrong. The seeing of a negative pattern for Kelly is predictive of the rest of her day, but when her mother points out that these may not be connected occurrences, this enables her to emotionally regulate and calm her thinking so that she is able to cope better. With her second child, the changing of priorities for Kelly is a positive coping strategy-

I think first time round that would have just stressed me out that I would have sort of noise and clothes all over the floor and things like that but then I just kind of flipped it on its head this time and thought well managing to feed a baby and look after a four year old and have a shower that's sort of quite an achievement rather than just being sort of a nightmare (Kelly).

This re-negotiation of her priorities enables her to be more accepting of her limitations and be able to appreciate what she can achieve. It feels a positive focus for her, rather than the focus on the unachievable.

Hazel has been able to identify activities that she can do that are calming for her-

For my quiet down time I do a lot of sort of sewing, cross-stitching and sewing and things like that and I guess and reading, I think I mentioned that to you, but I suppose sort of developing…. I think there is something about doing things with your hands, quite often that for me will certainly calm me down (Hazel).

It is a recognition of her own needs in this respect, a time for self, a time for calm. The physical repetitive craft that can aid the physiological calming of the body and doing something that she enjoys. It leads by example for her children, the ability to pursue calm activities that are productive or meet the needs of self.

Lynne who has three children under seven years old, reflects on her self-talk and realises that she needs to be more compassionate towards herself-

There have been times where I've said to.... like I've internally said stuff to myself and I've had that realisation of.... what are you.... kind of like what are you saying that for.... or what because you wouldn't dream of saying that to someone else in that situation (Lynne).

In terms of coping this reflective functioning is valuable. She realises that she would not speak to another person in such a negative way and she is able to challenge herself to be kinder to herself.

The lived experience of not coping can be experiences as difficult and unhappy, as Ava describes-

I had, had a really bad day, everything just made me cry (Ava).

Where as coping described here by Faye is a kinder happier experience-

I've achieved something and also I'm not overwhelmed, you know like that's a big achievement (Faye).

The experience of not coping can also impact the maternal infant relationship, as Beth relates here-

When I was at a bad time, I absolutely hated her, I really did (Beth).

Beth describes the experience of not coping and how it impacted how she felt towards her child. She continues here to comment on how she feels that society has expectations of motherhood that make it hard for her to comprehend how things could have been different for her-

I just felt completely overwhelmed all of the time and it was really really difficult. And it was really hard not to blame her for it even though it was me that did it, because I decided to bring her into the world, but I don't think (pause) I don't think, I don't think it would have been any other way if I had a different child or if I did things another way, because I think it's quite natural for women to put all this pressure on themselves to do it right because society expects them be independent and not to be expecting other people to drop in all the time and to make them meals and…. (Beth).

Beth highlights the expectations that the society around her place on mothers to be independent, to the detriment of mothers' coping abilities. This challenges the status quo in some ways and shows her insight into her own situation.

This first theme has introduced all of the mothers and gives examples of the extraordinary range of coping resources that they are able to call upon. It demonstrates the real and effective coping strategies that they are using on a daily basis. The inclusion of adaptive and potentially mal-adaptive strategies is significant in that the mothers are doing what they need to do to cope.

Coping was in many instances a very practical affair for the mothers, the problem-focused coping exampled by the mothers tending towards the soft- organisational strategies. There is a sense of needing to achieve something which offers a sense of 'my life is manageable'. These pragmatic and practical approaches ensure that they are supporting their ability to be successful and can achieve a sense of their own abilities, which can in turn support their mental and emotional well-being.

Linked to this, other forms of emotion focused coping that the mothers used, include support seeking, and expressions of emotional self-regulation such as "riding that wave" and "just walking away sometimes". We often make the choice of emotion focused coping when we think that a situation is one where nothing can be done to change things. While in contrast, problem focused coping is more likely to be used when we think that things can be changed for the better.

Recognition of personal choice and having realistic expectations are essentially self-reliant in nature and serve to support our emotional responses. It is an ethical response to being a parent in a way, protective of the child and effective adult functioning. Some cross over strategies like being in nature appear to be strategizing on the one hand but equally meet elements of emotional needs.

The reality of **not** coping for the mothers feels painful and detrimental to well-being. Where as coping is a kinder happier experience. The mothers in their accounts of the phenomenon of coping, show high levels of personal resourcefulness in terms of their emotional intelligence and their use of a wide variety of coping strategies that they have available to them. In the next chapter the mothers describe how they learn to care for themselves while being a mother; this is a difficult journey for them as they come to realise their own needs also need to be met.

Chapter Three

Learning the Importance of self-care

The mothers in this chapter describe an internal journey for them in terms of self-care and coping. This involves initially finding themselves low down on the hierarchy of needs, and then realising that they are unable to manage caring for their child if they do not meet some of their own needs. Beth describes finding herself at the "bottom of the pile" when she is using all her energy to try to be a better mother than her own.

> *I always promised myself I will be a better mother to my child than I had, and I feel like I wanted to do absolutely everything to ensure that we had a stable and perfect connection and I was so hell bent on that, that I caused extra pressure on myself, like I, for the first maybe five or six months of her life she spent it in my arms, which was what I thought you were supposed to do, because you know, my heart beat will calm her, what in fact that did was put me at the bottom of the pile* (Beth).

The recognition that she is at the bottom of the pile is then pivotal to enabling Beth to make changes to meet some of her needs. Beth is exhausted by her attempt to be a better mother than her own mother; she is desperate to remedy what was broken for her in her own experience. It feels as if this could make it better for her as well as her child if she can create the "perfect connection" with her child. There is a sense of righting a wrong almost, re-writing the past for her. Beth is thoughtful about self-care and challenges the thought that you can buy self-care for yourself-

> *I think that like, people think self-care, self-care is kind of this thing that you buy, but actually I think self-care is like choosing a course to do, or paying a bill, and making sure you are on top of life you know, not distracting yourself from it* (Beth).

This is sophisticated thinking in terms of coping and self-care; if she makes her life more manageable, she will be caring for herself in terms of her equilibrium, her life balance, and this will enhance her coping abilities.

She later describes how she has learnt to prioritise her own needs.

> *I'm developing as a human, and my highest level I have ever done, and part of that is because I'm a mum and that has its own stress, but part of it's because I'm doing something for me, like this evening I'm going to a singing lesson* (Beth).

Beth is taking some time for herself, to do something that she likes to do; this is valuable to her in terms of her own mind, finding time for her own joy and supporting her mental and emotional health.

In this next passage Dawn describes her experience of being "last down on the pecking order", she later explains further about not being able to look after herself, whilst still maintaining high standards for her baby-

> *Well I just looked like shit all the time, you know and I would always*

make sure that (child's) clothes were um.... I put something on insta-stories.... instagram the other day you know I got his little folded cardigan out and I got the little de-bobbling machine and everything making sure it's looking perfect and my own clothes I just.... pick it up off the floor, I just like.... I.... it's just covering my body and that will do, as long as he's not going... as long as he's clean and brushed and he's got all the things he needs and his needs met then I can just.... (sigh).... you know sometimes you feel like as a mother (pause) you are the child's shadow, that's how I felt like, and not actually.... sorry I'm going to start crying.... (Dawn).

Dawn's account of caring for her child's clothes to the utmost extent, even making sure there were no bobbles on his cardigan is in contrast with her attitude to her own clothes, which are picked up off the floor. The phrase "child's shadow" presents a feeling that Dawn feels that she is concealed from view, not noticed or not good enough; her needs are hidden and she is less worthy of care. Dawn is insightful in her reflection, but it visibly distresses her to hear it out loud and she has to stop. Dawn feels that she had to break before anyone recognised that she needed help.

> *But I feel like I had a breakdown I feel that I've had a breakdown before it got.... before we got.... I got....*(Dawn).

She struggles to express what she is trying to describe. The use of phrases like 'being broken', 'last down on the pecking order', 'bottom of the pile' by Dawn and Beth are strong and desperate, crying out for recognition of their needs. They come to a realisation that they themselves have to take action and meet their own needs.

Dawn tells how she has learnt to act as her own friend in this respect.

> *I just keep going through what I would be telling a friend, um I'm listening to happy things just trying to be practical and doing the leg work, going to the gym, yoga, reading, that all the people say you need to be doing, a healthy diet, getting out for fresh air, listening to happy things, just do all the stuff that people tell you to do* (Dawn).

For Dawn these activities that she undertakes to become well are work "doing the leg work". She is working at wellness and shows her ability to adapt and develop positive coping strategies. The ability to be your own friend appears incredibly positive for Dawn and relates back to positive rather than negative self-talk and the ability to be reflective of how we speak to ourselves. Dawn is able to listen to her inner knowledge about how to maintain her own mental health. She knows from her own experience what works for her, what is helpful and supportive for her. She has listened to advice from other people and has assimilated the things that work for her into it into the ability to help herself.

In a similar way to Dawn when she was unable to attend to the clothes she was wearing. Lynne also recognises a lack of interest in herself and how she looked-

> *I just didn't take much interest in how I looked particularly, I was just so so exhausted with (second child) when he was a baby, I just didn't have time to even consider how I looked half the time* (Lynne).

The exhaustion she felt limited her ability for self-care. Her energy is focused on caring for her baby. Another mother Isla also reflects that she was so concerned with providing care for her daughter that she did not look after herself "at all"-

> *I don't think I did, I really don't think I did look after myself at all, I think it was really um I was just much much more conscious of making sure she was ok* (Isla).

Isla contrasts her attentiveness to herself before and after having her child-

> *Before I had (child named) my hair would always be done, I had my make up on, now it like nah (laughs) scrape your hair back I've got no make-up on, if my clothes have anything less than poo on them, you know that's a win* (Isla).

There is a feeling of either/or here. It does not feel possible within their available resources to care for themselves and their babies; so in the mothers' protective stance, the infant becomes the priority to the detriment of self.

This pressure to be a perfect mother resonates with Hazel's account; there is a development for Hazel from trying so hard to be a perfect mum, to realising that she needs to develop kindness towards herself-

> *Learning to be kinder to myself um which I didn't in the beginning I really like I said for the first few months, sort of two months at least I felt like I needed to be perfect, I was putting so much pressure on myself* (Hazel).

For Hazel the transition to motherhood brings a realisation of the need to care for herself-

> *Definitely becoming a mum has taught me to kind of look after myself* (Hazel).

The risks of not doing so are a loss of self, a feeling of being used up and not replenished-

> *I can't put everybody else first before myself all the time because there will be nothing left of me* (Hazel).

The act of self-care in effect acts to restore the self, enabling the self to function: the lack of self-care affecting overall well-being, to the point of loss of self where there is "nothing left of me" (Hazel).

Isla reflects on something she was told by a family member-

> *Well my granddad always used to say…. you can't pour from an empty cup…. so there is no point running yourself into the ground repeatedly* (Isla).

Isla is able to rationalize that she will be better able to care for her daughter if she is able to take care of her own needs-

> *Actually I'm going to come back and be a happier, nicer person (laughs) a more patient person, um and that's better for her….* (Isla).

This recognition is protective of the child, providing a more balanced ability to provide care for her child; and also acknowledges her limitations as a person.

The placing self at the bottom of the hierarchy of needs is an ongoing issue for Jinny-

> *Right at the bottom, yes it was always…. it was always the children first, my partner, then me and I think that's still the case now actually* (Jinny).

However in some way Jinny knows that self-care is important if only to be able to continue caring for others-

> *I think as we get older it definitely becomes more clear to us that we need to be ok ourselves before we can look after others* (Jinny).

There is a feeling that having a sense of well-being in herself, enables Jinny to endow well-being in her children. This demonstrates a sophisticated reflexive reasoning that is something Jinny attributes to her life experience.

Kelly reflects on attitude to self and showing self-appreciation for the mental and physical challenges of bringing up children for both parents-

> *It's a really big thing, it's a big life style change and it takes a lot out of you both physically and mentally, um it's a positive thing like you are bringing up a child but you know some people probably underestimate that and definitely I think mums make themselves feel worse by the fact that you know apart from your own family a lot of people around you don't really appreciate that it's a massive thing that you're going through* (Kelly).

This mental attitude of self-appreciation is supportive and benefits from being non-judgmental and acceptant of the struggles that are common to motherhood and fatherhood. It is obvious that motherhood is 'normal' but the strains are interpreted as unappreciated by others here, and giving self-credit for what you can is self-caring in this respect. It lessens the need to strive for the unachievable perfection.

Lynne recognises that she needs to monitor her 'self-talk' in a light of recognising the need for self-compassion-

> *Because there have been times where I've said to.... like I've internally said stuff to myself and I've had that realisation of.... what are you.... kind of like what are you saying that for.... or what because you wouldn't dream of saying that to someone else in that situation* (Lynne).

This is also recognition of the need for self-care. It is emotional care-taking of the self, as you would for someone that you loved. The journey from elements of self-neglect and being bottom of the hierarchy of needs for the mothers appears to be one of self-realisation that they cannot function in a balanced way of coping without the ability to meet some of their own basic needs. This realisation appears to be part of the journey into motherhood that in a way is quite a normal thing for all mothers. As mothers we do our best to look after and protect our babies and this can come at a cost to self.

In the next chapter the mothers talk about how they learn to manage the change to their identity and take care of themselves. Half of the mothers were interviewed a second time and were able to give an insight into how they found trying to maintain elements of self-care in their lives. Dawn here refers back to her initial interview and says that she has tried to prioritise self-care on an on-going basis-

> *I've been working hard on.... on what we talked about.... working hard on um building myself up again um and um recognising who I am or who I was and who I am outside of being a mother you know.... um making that space and just um chipping away at self care, that's.... that's been high up my priority list really* (Dawn).

Dawn had described feeling "broken" in her initial interview. She explained, "I've lost (pause) who I was". The ability to validate her identity again, outside of motherhood, feels like a healthy redirection for Dawn in terms of her coping strategies. She is rebuilding her sense of self and personhood and making a space for herself in the world. Her attempts to recognise who she was as a person and who she is now, whilst knowing that she is also a mother, suggests that she needs to integrate the different aspects of herself as a person. Dawn is re-writing her story, re-integrating parts of the whole. It is hard work for her and challenging, and it is done by making small improvements "chipping away at self-care". She is making progress in her ability to prioritise her own needs so that she is not "bottom of the pile" as she had previously felt.

Chloe relates meeting her own needs with her ability to be able to parent, she realises that if she does not meet any of her own needs she will be unable to function in other ways. She talks here of burn out, resonating with Dawn's description of being "broken"-

> *I think I'm doing a much better job of that I think I got to a point where I really was burning myself out, and I've kind of gone .... actually ....*

sometimes it has to put me first…. because if I don't put me first I can't do all of the other things (Chloe).

This level of debilitation that the mothers describe signifies feelings of emptiness and mental, physical and emotional exhaustion. Like Dawn she relates meeting her needs with identity outside of motherhood-

Having something to focus on that was something that really mattered to me that was outside of being mum all of the time because I think sometimes it feels like the hardest job in the world being a mum, because the people you are being a mum to are not always grateful for the things that you do (Chloe).

There is a sense of the struggle for her. Parenting is hard and there is a lack of recognition of her efforts.

Beth identifies that she is maintaining the self-care activities that she had put into place-

For self care like swimming, singing and painting and stuff because that's all stuff that I do now even still….(Beth).

These activities relate to her needs as a person and are not specific to her as a mother. The recognition that she still does them indicates that they are valued by her and are meeting her needs in the recognition of her as a person outside of motherhood.

Dawn again describes the hard work of maintaining wellness, working at mental health and being able to enjoy her life. Dawn uses humour to help herself-

I am working really hard at doing as much as I can to enjoy life again really and having the stand-up comedy the funny audio books ready to go so I can put them in so I force myself to listen to them to get.... to find.... to pull out a laugh or something (Dawn).

This laughter, although hard to find helps her, perhaps in gaining perspective or maybe just a physiological boost of energy.

Ellie recognises this too, the need to do things that are meeting some of her own needs.

I realised why 'me' time is important so whereas before I wouldn't really try and do anything by myself because I would feel guilty about it, like the kids go to bed they are asleep any way so now I might have a bath or I'm sewing again so I might do some sewing or read a book and I don't feel bad for it anymore so in that aspect my mental health is better because I understand that.... yes I do need time to just be me.... (Ellie).

The fact that her children are older now and less dependent seems to have helped. Ellie is more able to find time for self-care, having a "bath", but also activities that she enjoys for herself. These activities support her identity and in consequence of this, her mental health also. They are simple activities of sewing and reading but for Ellie it reinforces the "me" in her. The "me" is an identity outside of motherhood for Ellie who previously recalled naming herself purely in terms of her relationship to her children. Ellie recognises a loss of the "me" that she was, but is trying to reclaim part of her previous identity-

I don't think I'm ever going to be the me that I was but it would be nice to be a bit of me again so.... so I can say when people say.... who are you.... I can say well I'm (name) I'm (children named) mum, I'm (name) ... rather than the other way around (Ellie).

The ability to name herself again is an important step in regaining her mental equanimity and her ability to express herself as an individual and to know what she wants for herself in her own life. The loss of self for Ellie has bordered on depersonalization and may have indicated a maladaptive coping for her of mental withdrawal. However, the adaptive element is important as it can be acknowledged for her, that it may have helped her get through her most difficult times.

Faye is reflective about her ability to meet her own needs-

> *I don't have to be super mum all the time, that just being (child named) mum is enough for her and that she's happy, loved, secure and sometimes it's nice for her as well to have some downtime and not be constantly engaged um I suppose that I'm not a bad mum for allowing a little bit extra whatever it is or not constantly doing things um yes I just say the same to myself really that I'm not a bad mum for putting myself first for a little bit, because that allows me to be a good mum for her* (Faye).

Faye reflects that her daughter's needs are being met and that it is helpful to her as a mother to be able to put her own needs first at times. This complex balancing of activity time and down time for her daughter appears to bring up feelings of worthiness as a mother in Faye. However, she is able to reflectively examine her own beliefs, judgments and practices and concludes that the ability to meet some of her own needs enhances her abilities as a mother.

The struggle for the mothers to be able to maintain and prioritise meeting some of their own needs appears to be ongoing in some respects. It may be mitigated to some extent by the developing independence of their children and the recognition of the difficulty in caring for others if you are unable to care for yourself. The ability to meet their own needs is recognised as supportive to coping, and protective of the children. As Chloe says, "because if I don't put me first I can't do all of the other things". However as Dawn identifies the ability to maintain levels of self-care requires on-going effort and work.

This second theme *Learning the importance of self-care* details the journey for the mothers from elements of self-neglect and being bottom of the hierarchy of needs, to one of self- realisation that they cannot function in a balanced way of coping, without the ability to meet some of their own needs. Achieving balance in life is complicated, we require energy to be able to carry out what needs to be done in our lives and we also require relaxation. Equilibrium is not the absence of either of these but rather a balancing of the two. Maslow (1954, 2011) explains "Homeostasis means coming not to zero but to an optimum level. This means sometimes reducing tension, sometimes increasing it" (p.33).

When we consider what this means for mothers, it would seem obvious that there are stresses, but these are not all negative and many may be pleasurable. However the recognition of the need for rest and relaxation does not always appear so apparent in mother's or in children's lives today. Children however can provide many opportunities for rest as they sleep more than adults; but if we are active when they are resting, we may be denying ourselves and them, opportunities for really restorative co-regulation and rest. The need to maintain high standards of order in domestic and working environments when looking after young children can negatively impact our ability to rest and restore our balance and equilibrium. Maybe at times it can appear that we are just trying too hard, doing too much, and it can be our mental health that suffers.

However Kurki (2020) suggests that self-care is an ethical duty. As individuals we are governed by freedom of choice, taking care of ourselves entails listening to oneself, reflecting on what we need and acting on those needs. For the mothers the needs of their vulnerable new-born infants for a while are placed higher than their own. The role of family and community can be influential in this struggle and there may be effects on the mothers seen from the decline of family networks and cohesive neighbourhoods that can support new mothers in more traditional family systems.

Additionally Stokes (1981) suggests that self-care practices are a health resource for individuals. Some of the mothers suggest that they learnt self-care practices from learning about the care needs of their children. Our knowledge about our own care needs may be variable and based on individual's experiences of being cared for. The expressions of self-care through attention to a healthy diet, rest and exercise balance, mental and spiritual fulfilment is potentially a lifelong path of learning, which can be accentuated by childbirth and child-care requirements.

Self- compassion can be described as self-kindness. The inter-connected nature of the ability to self-care appears complex and challenging for new mothers who are at a particularly vulnerable time in their lives where the nature of motherhood involves the transfer of resources from the self to the child (Bardake, 2012).

Chapter Four

Losing selfhood-reclaiming selfhood

Many research studies have found that self-care abilities and self-compassion are found to be strongly linked to emotional well-being, with self-compassion being significantly correlated with positive mental health outcomes including lower rates of depression and anxiety and improved life satisfaction (Bogels, Hellemans, Van Deursen, Romer, & Van der Meulen, 2014; Germer & Neff, 2015; Neff, 2003). In this respect having self-compassion and the ability to care for the self would be a positive mental health strategy that could support coping. For the mothers, the ability to be able to 'take care of yourself', appears to be wrapped up in identity. Identity was a difficult issue for them and one in which they predominantly expressed a sense of loss. The concept of selfhood is based around the quality of self that constitutes individuality as a person (Oxford Essential English Dictionary, 2011).

Beth expresses a loss of some positive aspects of her personality-

> *I think, I've always been quite a positive person, but motherhood made me incredibly negative all of the time* (Beth).

However, we can question if this is motherhood or the mental ill-health that came with motherhood for Beth. She later returns to this sense of loss, of "losing" who she is and having to re-invent herself-

I've always been absolutely fine with who I am but, I really struggled with- because you don't know who you are when you are a mum, for the first time, you absolutely don't, everything changes, every part of you that you enjoyed before disappears for some reason. Then it takes such a long time for that to come back, because you have to re-invent yourself, you have to say goodbye to the person that you were before, completely and then re-build your life (Beth).

Beth assumes that her experience is felt by others, "you don't know who you are when you are a mum" and this raises a lot of questions: why does motherhood obliterate who she feels she is beforehand; is this a common experience for mothers; why has everything changed for her; what do mothers need, to be able to maintain a sense of coherent identity that transitions childbirth?

The re-building of her life and identity is a positive feature in her narrative, but she is cautionary to herself for the future. She does not want to go through the experience of losing herself again. This loss for her is serious and risky-

I never want to sacrifice myself like that again, it's not worth it really, but the journey that I've been on, and however much I've come out of it and developed, it could have quite easily gone the other way, you know and I don't want to put myself at risk like that…. we just sometimes seem to forget that your mental health is incredibly important and it can be the choice like between life and death or completely suffering or not (Beth).

Through this experience of losing herself and suffering, Beth seems to learn that she needs to be able to prioritise her mental health needs. For Beth the experience was life threatening and the knowledge she gains is the importance of her ability to maintain her mental health.

Ellie remarks that when she is asked who she is "I always go (children named) mum" and at the time this seems to be enough for her. However, motherhood is demanding of time and energy and creates difficulties for mothers in terms of remembering who they are and that their needs are legitimate.

Faye uses the word "just" as she explains that she is a full-time mum-

> *I'm just a full time mum and obviously stuck in the house…* (Faye).

When the word "just" is challenged she replies-

> *Yes I know, um it's a bit of a weird one, I think…. I think people put a lot of um merit on having a job rather than staying at home, as a mum…. so I find that hard….* (Faye).

Faye implies that merit is given to paid work and that motherhood does not attract this same merit; the significance is in how she then feels about herself, in a way less valuable and maybe less valued. Faye communicates that she thinks this is unfair. However the consequences are that she feels that her identity as a stay-at-home mother is not as valued as working mothers, and she feels "stuck".

Dawn differentiates between losing her identity and losing who she was as a person, but it is unclear whether it is motherhood or poor mental health that is causing this feeling, although both appear interlinked for Dawn-

I feel like my um I've lost my.... not my identity but I've lost (pause)
who I was, um the laid back, chilled sort of person, I feel like I'm always
pretty uptight just waiting for the next bad thing to happen. (Dawn).

Dawn goes on to describe herself as her baby's shadow, indicating
the lack of self-worth that she feels. She is there to make sure things
are done for her baby, but you get a sense of her loss of self-

You're existing but um he is my life now and I'm just a sort of a shadow,
attached to him, making sure that everythings, everythings done (Dawn).

For Dawn her ability to return to work was critical for a return to
a sense of her own individuality and her rights in her world. It
suggests a memory of a more certain time for her when she knew
who she was as a person, and when she was able to be self-sufficient
financially. She says-

I should have gone back to work sooner and insisted.... so, then I'd have
had money and I'd have been working as well so I wasn't just yes I wish
I'd got the balance back sooner, and I think that would have helped my
mentality....my mentality.... my state of mind as well, I deserve my
space in the world.... (Dawn).

This use of the term "deserve my space in the world" is loaded with
meaning. There is a sense that she feels that this has been denied
her, a feeling of inequality, a feeling that she needs to be heard and
that she has a right to be heard. Then she would be able to re-
balance, re-establish equanimity for herself and heal. The need
for financial independence is evident here in connection with her
understanding of balance in her own life. Dawn says she should
have "insisted" fought for her right to choose to work if that's what

she needed. There is a feeling that the expectation of society around her was that mothers do not return to work in the first few months after having a baby, and that this was restrictive of her free choice to make her own decision in the matter.

It seems that being able to maintain or re-create an identity that provides a sense of coherence and balance is important for the mothers, in terms of having the ability to meet their own needs. Lynne also describes a loss of self-

> *I just completely lost myself I just wasn't the person that I used to be* (Lynne).

This is the self that belongs to the 'me' in us all, 'myself', not the part of self that relates to other people-

> *I just felt like I didn't have any interests myself, that's the only way I can describe it, I think literally…. I think particularly after (second child) it just felt like an existence, that's the only way I can describe it as just getting though the best I could* (Lynne).

The loss of activities and interests that would have been pursued prior to motherhood appears significant here. It feels like an existence "just getting through" (Lynne), not living a life which is fulfilling-

> *I describe that feeling of when I'm feeling really detached and I had that feeling with both* (children)(Lynne).

This feeling of detachment suggests a feeling of emotional numbing or exhaustion. It is possibly protective in some ways in terms of coping but it is also passive and helpless to some extent. Later Lynne is able to pursue some interests for herself and this is helpful for her need to regain her sense of self-

> *I did do two courses when I was on my maternity leave with (children named) that probably helped because it gave me um something for me* (Lynne).

This doing of something for 'me' helping to replenish the sense of selfhood that had been lost.

Grace here describes an absolute clash of expectation versus reality. She explains with humour how her expectations of early motherhood were not grounded in reality-

> *You don't actually understand … what you do all day long, like I remember planning to paint the house whilst I was on maternity leave and now that seems completely insane to think that that would have been something that you would have been able to do, I don't know where I pictured the children were (laughs) do you know? Erm so yes it was probably a bit…. I don't think I realised how erm intense it maybe was and I think especially when they are very young, it's quite um it can be quite boring as well,* (Grace).

The reality of her parenting experiences are clearly expressed here as all absorbing, intense, time consuming, boring at times with repetitive tasks and not in alignment with her pre-parenting expectations. The humour she expresses feels healthy in response to the dramatic clash between expectation and reality, but there is also a level of distress and a loss of self.

> *I feel like I'm coming back to feeling more like myself now but um yes because I think that I've always been somebody who has been quite*

confident um and um very decisive and I've always had quite a good memory, and those three things were quite significantly impacted, and that was very strange.... I think the real.... the kind of judgments you get really knocks your confidence and then just the tiredness just really knocks your memory and then I couldn't make a decision to save my life (**Grace**).

The confident, decisive person who was able to remember important details was then unable to make decisions and became self-doubting and not confident in what she was doing. Tiredness appears as debilitating, making it hard for her to manage her daily life, but the loss of self is perhaps more significant, the person who is known to the self, being no longer there.

For Hazel there are massive changes felt in her sense of identity, but they are more positive for her-

I feel like (child named) changed the essence of who I am really like how I feel about myself, how my priorities in life changed, it kind of all.... not made sense, but kind of shifted into a much kind of.... I think calmer pattern for me rather than being all focused on work and studying and everything like that (**Hazel**).

This change in the "essence" of her being indicates something abstract but self-determining, a powerful shift of priorities and peaceful in its 'calming'. There is a sense that her life has become more understandable for her with the birth of her child. We do not know if these shifts in life priorities are permanent or flowing with the changing needs of her infant.

For Isla there is a challenge of her confidence in her own abilities and competencies-

I think because of the perfectionist issues that I have, nothing I ever do is ever good enough, um and I think that regardless of what your personality is like I think being a mum makes you question everything that you do, um you know…. am I doing it right (Isla).

This feels like a loss for her and there is a need to re-balance her sense of coherence, that her life is manageable. She seems to do this by doing things that interest her that are not about being a mum-

I would give my last breath for her if that's what she needed…. but I also am me um I have things that I'm interested in that don't link to being a mum (Isla).

This statement "I also am me" is profound. She is a mother to her child but there is a feeling that she is struggling to integrate her motherhood with her self-identity. The part of her that is a mother is more of a generic sense of motherhood and not specific to her as an individual. Isla develops this thought later-

You can't be everything to everyone, and you need to…. to be something to yourself sometimes (Isla).

The word "be" in this context may infer ideas around existence: to live and breathe, to consider self. If you meet everyone else's needs, you leave nothing left of yourself. The necessity to meet her own needs in terms of her identity and the integrity of her personality seems clearly stated here.

Jinny also recognises a need in herself to return to work-

I imagined I would be so in love with this baby and I would want to do everything with…. with this baby, but in reality I just wanted to get back to work, because that was my norm and that was where I ….where I was comfortable I think (Jinny).

It feels as if work for Jinny is a safe place where she is able to understand her role and feel at ease. She has confidence in her work identity and her abilities, to meet the expectations of her as a person. Later in Jinny's story, she relates that the key phase for alerting her partner when she is not ok is "I'm not feeling myself". The statement implies that this is when she is not able to feel or behave in a way that is normal for her, or in a way that she recognises as her usual self. This reflective ability to recognise this changed internal state is pivotal to her coping abilities. It is this ability that enables her to seek support appropriately to meet her needs and return to an internal state of equilibrium where she can recognise herself again.

Jinny's experience resonates with Kelly's description of losing her sense of identity, and feeling a need to return to work where she knew who she was and had a support network of friends-

When I got the post-natal depression, I think I had sort of really lost my own identity I felt like I was just a mum, I didn't do any of the things that I used to do, obviously you know, the big thing was that I wasn't at work anymore and that a lot of my life and probably a lot of my social life did centre around my colleagues and things (Kelly).

Kelly describes post-natal depression with the preposition "the", as if it is a generalised illness not specific for her. There is a sense that she does not wish to identify herself with it. If Kelly had difficulty feeling valuable to her own child at times, it could in the same way make it more difficult for her to value herself as a mother. However, for Kelly the loss of identity appears in some ways to be a symptom of her post-natal depression. She recognises the loss of the things that she used to do, that were bound up with her identity before motherhood. The phrase "I was just a mum" resonates with Faye's description of "I'm just a full time mum" and signifies a feeling of loss, maybe a loss of status, maybe a loss of social and financial security, possibly a feeling of not being as valued? For Kelly there is a need to reclaim all of these elements of her life, in order to reclaim her identity.

The complexity of maintaining identity through the transition to motherhood is evident. Who you are, the way that you think about yourself and the way that others view you are all essential characteristics of identity and are essentially bound up with coping. The additional burden of mental ill-health is significant in the struggle to maintain a coherent sense of identity for these mothers. The necessity of meeting some of their own needs as individuals in their own right, outside of motherhood, appears pivotal for them.

The mothers describe a transition into motherhood that involves their changing concepts of selfhood. The palpable sense of loss for some with the use of terms such as "shadow" (Dawn), expresses a real struggle to maintain a sense of cohesive identity. A research study by Laney, Lewis Hall, Anderson and Willingham (2015) which looked at the influences of motherhood on women's identity, found that women lost themselves for a while whist incorporating children into their identity, this seems to fit with the experience of the mothers in this study. There is an initial stress and inability to focus on self-care needs, followed by recognition of their need for this. Laney et al. (2015) describe the mother's expansion of self, which develops as children are incorporated into the woman's identity and self-boundaries. The loss of the previous self, before motherhood occurs as the mother transitions to include her children into her concepts of selfhood.

The additional complexity of mental ill-heath and motherhood may make it more difficult for mothers. Mental health difficulties can also involve a loss of self in some respects; identity theory suggests that self-concepts are constructed through self-awareness (Hine, Maybery & Goodyear, 2018). When we think about ourselves, we become the thinker and the subject of the thought and this is constitutes self-consciousness or self-awareness (Aroosi, 2019). It is not a static phenomenon rather it changes in response to environment and social context (Hine et al., 2018).

Linked to this Coffey (2003) writes that recovery in terms of mental illness is concerned with reclaiming a sense of personhood which can transcend thinking of oneself as just being mentally ill. Motherhood has the potential to transform a women's identity in a positive way by creating a sense of meaning and connection that over time can increase confidence, providing a healthy life focus and sense of normality in everyday life and creating meaning and a role outside of mental health difficulties.

Personal recovery is found to be bound up in how we function in life as a whole. This includes how we engage with others socially and our sense of agency for self, the subjective feeling of controlling our own actions and through this what happens to us (Hine et al., 2018). The fact of having a child to advocate for may give women this sense of agency. The ability to plan and carry out care of an infant gives that understanding of life as meaningful that Antonovsky (1996) talks of as our sense of coherence. The mothers strive to re-gain some balance in their lives that can meet the needs of their children as well as their own needs. Re-establishing time for their own interests is important and helps them reclaim a sense of self and individual identity.

Allen (2005) argues that we as individuals need to devote as much energy into learning how to feel good as we do about feeling bad. Pain and negative emotions are able to guide us in what we need to avoid, but in the same way our positive emotions can guide us to activities that lead to our growth and development. Making good experiences part of our daily routine and meeting our basic needs of nutrition, rest, exercise, social, mental and spiritual wellbeing are part of valuing ourselves. This taking care of yourself implies valuing yourself. These are probably the pivotal challenges for mothers who have mental ill-health. They are being protective of their infants by prioritising the infant's needs. However, the realisation of the need to meet their own needs and taking steps to do this is an absolute necessity for achieving balance and wellness and the ability to cope in their everyday lives and ultimately this protects the child. During this time of transition, the importance of engaging with others within supportive contexts cannot be underestimated.

In the next chapter the mothers discuss for them what support is helpful to them and what is not. It is often a subtle delineation.

Chapter Five

Identifying effective support

For mothers the losing a sense of selfhood discussed in the previous chapter is a challenging process. Their horizons expand to incorporate their children and re-balance into a new sense of selfhood. During this time the importance of engaging with others within supportive contexts cannot be underestimated. Effective support can be considered to be any action by a person that is successful in providing mental, physical or emotional assistance to another person in a time of need.

Beth describes how her husband was able to support her emotionally through his acceptance of her. The question asked is "What makes you feel cared for?". She takes a long time to think about her answer at the beginning of the passage and then describes beautifully what it is that he does that helps her-

> *(Long pause) erm probably acceptance from my husband more than anything, I know that sounds silly but, I think I was really angry all the time and I was really exhausted all the time so, just having somebody that just didn't get offended by that or just didn't take it personally that you know sometimes that I was going to struggle and that means more than anything, that helps more than anything, to know that I am secure, and to know that I am safe, and that, even though I am going through a hard time I've still got somebody that just accepts me for who I am and whatever happens you know that underneath it all, that it's ok, he's still going to be there for me* (Beth).

Beth articulates her feelings of anger and exhaustion interposed with feelings of safety that come from her husband's ability to communicate acceptance of her as a person. He is non-judgmental of her struggle and does not make it about himself by taking things personally or getting offended. This acts as an emotional 'holding' for her and supports her from descending into more negative realms. The giving of this emotional support lifts her sense of coping in terms of 'my world is understandable'. The feeling of safety that Beth receives from her husband's ability to communicate this acceptance to her, helps her feel that her world is more manageable and supports her overall sense of coherence and her ability to understand her world.

Ava describes the effective support that she received from her partner when she is starting to get back to doing normal things like driving the car after having her baby. It might sound like gentle encouragement to an outsider, but for her it is "tough love", and it is the push that she needs. She recalls her partner saying to her-

> *'Just go out and do it, do it while you can, just go round the block that's all you need to do'. But I think if I didn't have that bit of a push with those little things, I'd have really struggled and it would have turned out to be bigger problems and bigger things, that tough love helped* (Ava).

This must be a difficult line to draw for partners. It is obviously scary for Ava to drive the car with her baby in it for the first time, a feeling that would resonate with many parents. The enormity of responsibility that descends with the birth of a child, perhaps with a first child in particular. The line between effective support and being overbearing might be relationship dependent and takes sensitivity on behalf of Ava's partner. He supports her sense of coherence in her life in terms of its manageability.

For Ava being able to manage and get on with the little things in life that loomed large for her helped her cope in a wider sense. It achieved a sense of agency for her that brought with it a feeling of being capable that contributed to her well-being. It was important that the "tough love" was loving however, and that it came from a supportive stance from her husband and was therefore not perceived as undermining or unhelpful.

A small act of kindness by her husband is recounted by Chloe. She describes it as "really valuable". The "small act" appears to signal to Chloe that she is being thought about, when she herself has to spend so much of her time and energy on thinking about others and in particular the needs of her children throughout the rest of the day-

> *It's a feeling of I was thinking of you, you know, and he does things like he brings me a cup of tea every morning, and it's just a really small act but it's something that, is really valuable to my day, it's a really lovely way to start my day, with somebody saying this is something that I can do for you* (Chloe).

There is another element in effective support for Chloe as her husband shows that he is able to hold her in mind when he goes to work-

> *I think he is very good at acknowledging how I am feeling and asking me about that rather than dismissing it or ignoring it. So, he can sort of sense that I've had a bad day or a bad day is brewing and if I've had a*

difficult morning before he's left, he'll message me later on and say' how are you doing' and that makes me feel cared for (Chloe).

He is able to acknowledge her difficult emotions and offer support through his remembering and inquiring about how she is 'doing'. There is a sense too that she is feeling accepted and not judged in this account, and she feels cared for in this respect.

Chloe identifies that for her being listened to, is helpful, but she does not like it if someone jumps in to help her when she has not asked them to-

> *So in terms of being helpful, I think one of the most helpful things is when people ask what they can do to help, or ask how you are feeling and listen, rather than jumping in and trying to fix the situation or offering advice that hasn't been asked for in the first place* (Chloe).

This ability to listen to someone without trying to fix them or the situation they are in really resonates. Often, we may want to work out our own solutions and just need a sounding board or a listening ear. This is supportive and does not undermine any capability that we may have or leave us with the impression that we need fixing. It is empowering.

Dawn identifies the difficulty of not being on the same page as her husband in terms of childcare and how this impacts her regarding effective support-

> *My husband will just keep giving him milk, so we are not quite on the same page as to what to try and do, my husband's getting better, um because now he's doing night shifts as well* (Dawn).

Dawn's baby was waking "15-20 times in the night" and until her husband was taking a turn at childcare at night, they were not able to parent in a joined-up way. In her narrative she describes repeatedly that she had to 'break' before it was noticed that she needed help.

Her ability to cope was assumed in spite of the severe sleep deprivation that she encountered. There was an impression for her that as a mother she was expected to be able to cope, Dawn is clear about how she feels about this-

> *When a woman's had a baby, because women just push through and battle on because you think that's what everyone else is doing and you think that's what I should be doing being the bottom of the pile, you know women are cracking and imagine when women are having babies I find that women are already working the hardest they can, they are already at full capacity, between work and being expected to be this person and be that person and then you have a baby on top of that and it's just oh my god you know, so yes that motherhood yes* (Dawn).

The expectation is from her as a woman as well as from others around her and this has implications for society's attitudes to supporting new parents. Dawn appears to accept that her husband is not different from society as a whole in his assumption that she can cope with what is in realistic terms the impossible. It takes his experiencing of 'doing the night shift' with their baby for him to be able to 'be on the same page' in terms of their joint parenting and to be able to validate her need for support.

For Dawn the multiple roles and demands on women in society already place women in a vulnerable position. Her description of being "this person and be that person" suggests that women have multiple identities that make demands on them. The recognition that she deserves for being a mother does not appear to be an easy gain for her and there are serious losses for her in terms of her well-being before she starts her recovery. Her husband's support when it does come is transformative for her and as she is then able to develop a voice and express her own needs as she explains here "I am asking for more help now as well" (Dawn).

Ellie explains how she values her husband's encouragement to get out and do something different when she has had a bad day during the week-

> *It usually ends up being that typically the bad days are a weekday and then the weekend we've got (husband) and we go out and do something and it's really good and it sort of snaps me out of it* (Ellie).

This going out and doing something different is helpful for Ellie and supports her coping abilities, she suggests that it can alter her mood and make her feel better in herself.

Support from other people who are external to the household comes from multiple sources through relationships with family members, friends, parenting groups, work colleagues. Faye describes a friendship that surprises her in its ability to support her, as it comes from a woman who does not have children-

> *I've got friends, older friends who've actually been fantastic, um since I've given birth, and I think its made our friendships stronger, um and friends actually…. one of my friends doesn't even like children, and she's been*

fantastic, you know she's been the best one at really like checking in with me and making sure that I'm ok and asking about the baby (Faye).

The act of 'checking in' is valuable for Faye, it is not so much about doing, but of asking the questions from a standpoint of genuine interest that is the supportive factor, and Faye has confidence in the genuineness of the support as she feels there is no other motive present.

Ellie describes attending baby groups and how this helped her to connect with other mothers, forming a close friendship with another mum that has lasted-

I went to loads of groups with (child named), and I kept in touch with all of them, and we've all got a second one around the same age now so I've got one that I class as a really good friend and I've got a couple of others, you know, that I'm quite happy to go out for coffee and stuff (Ellie).

Attendance of baby groups was mainly mentioned by the mothers in a supportive context. However for some mothers it was an added pressure with which they had difficulty coping. In this passage Beth describes her experience of attending groups-

You've got to go to groups because there is that pressure that you, you know, you are supposed to go and do that, when actually if you've got anxiety issues which a lot of people do, when they have a baby, that isn't always the best environment for them to be in. Like for me I used to go to groups and then spend half my time crying, because I just couldn't talk to anyone, and my baby couldn't talk, and I just felt like, what am I doing here, I don't like anybody really (laughs) (Beth).

This passage is deeply expressive. Beth almost finds it laughable that she can't talk to anyone, and neither can her baby, so what is she doing there. She articulates that it may not be the right place for someone who is feeling raised levels of anxiety.

For Dawn also it represented a struggle and a pressure to attend groups-

> *Mother and toddler groups? Um yes I sort of did but I just…. this ahh…. I just felt really exposed umm… Yes and you know in all fairness my husband's friends, wives and girlfriends were saying come on come out to these groups, you know I could never relax around them and I thought no you know that's no good* (Dawn).

Dawn was unable to relax in the group environment, feeling exposed and uncomfortable she takes the decision not to go. Dawn describes how she feels as people constantly tried to advise her what to do to help her baby sleep better-

> *When you are already doubting yourself, somebody giving…. my, my and it's my issue when somebody is giving me advice I think they think I don't know what I'm doing, and I…. that's always been… because I've always been capable I suddenly thought to myself I'm not capable* (Dawn).

There is considerable dysfluency in this passage characterised by the involuntary repetition of "my" and changes in flow and rhythm, as Dawn appears to grapple with intense emotions. These emotions leave her feeling vulnerable and not up to meeting up with people that might offer her advice, advise that makes her feel that she doesn't know what she is doing and makes her question herself.

Nevertheless, she is able to gain support from a social media App for mothers who are awake in the night with their babies. Dawn explains that it is able to alleviate feelings of loneliness for her when she is up alone at night with her baby-

> *There's stuff like little stories and a forum just so people can say 'hi, anyone else awake out there?' you know, it's quite new because that's when people tend to feel the loneliness* (Dawn).

The feeling that she is not alone in her night-time vigil is supportive in the way that her world is understandable and therefore can be manageable.

In terms of ineffective support, Grace like Dawn finds unsolicited advice very difficult to manage at times-

> *I don't like getting advice unless I've asked for it, yes that drives me insane* (Grace).
> *With (second child) thankfully, I um started to have a bit of um a filter for the unwanted advice* (Grace).

Grace is adamant that unsolicited advice is not helpful. However she is able in time to build resilience through the development of experience-based confidence, and by her second child she has developed a filter for unsolicited advice which is protective for her in terms of her coping. Faye similarly differentiates between asked for advice and unsolicited advice, which she finds difficult and almost as if she is not really being heard when all she wants is to complain a little-

> *So I think if I ask for advice and it's given, I think that's really helpful,*

but I think when people offer advice without being asked um not so.... not so helpful, just because sometimes I just want to complain to somebody um it doesn't mean I want their opinion on how I should be doing it differently (Faye).

However, Grace recognises both social and practical support as helpful to her-

So like when people had come, but like coming and sitting and hanging around with you, and maybe like cleaning, or my Dad both times, he came over when (child named) was born for I think two weeks, and he made all of our meals for the two weeks (Grace).

The impact of providing meals for new parents has been mentioned repeatedly by mothers as really effective in reducing the strains in early parenthood. Hazel echo's this, for her the gift of cooked meals is incredibly valuable in terms of support in the early days of caring for her baby-

(Husband's) parents cooked us I think a month's worth of meals so freshly cooked meals to go in our freezer, I still remember it now, I think I can still remember the taste of them and they were just such a godsend to us (Hazel).

Another practical aspect of effective support is mentioned by Jinny when her sister will take the children for a few hours-

So my sister, everything she does is helpful…. she'll maybe have them once a week for me and it isn't planned and its quite a nice surprise when she does it, she'll just pick them up from school for me and take them home to dinner and have them for a few hours, and maybe a sleep over on the weekends (Jinny).

It is not everyone who has this level of family support and Jinny acknowledges it as valuable. It is enabling of rest and restore time for parents and supportive in this way of overall coping abilities.

The effectiveness of practical support is exampled by Kelly here when her close family are able to help her-

> *They know that what you really need is sort of the practical stuff like you know, to grab all of your dirty washing and put it in for the baby* (Kelly).

This relieving of the practical burdens of childcare are able to lift the burden of care away from the mother so that she potentially is able to relax and enjoy the baby.

However, it is a fine line between effective support and intrusive ineffective support-

> *My mother-in-law would kind of take the baby out of the room and say…. you need to get some sleep we will look after the baby…. and stuff but after the birth I was quite anxious for a couple of weeks, um and looking back on it now, I just didn't sleep when the baby wasn't with me* (Kelly).

This well-meaning intervention was unsuccessful, and it would indicate that the use of checking questions might be able to differentiate effective from ineffective support, asking 'would it be helpful if…' and not making assumptions might in this way be recommended.

Talking about what she finds hard is initially difficult for Isla in her WhatsApp friendship group, the day-to-day difficulties in caring for a tiny child, but when they were able to share these things it became incredibly helpful as a means of expression and support-

> *All the normal things that I think everyone goes through, but um I can't get her to go to sleep or you know I've had three poo explosions this week I'm at the end of my tether and I can't do any more washing, that sort of stuff…. but um kind of the important stuff* (Isla).

These day-to-day events are the familiar experiences of early parenting but constitute the "important stuff" for Isla in terms of what needs to be coped with. The ability to express and share frustrations is enabling for Isla. The use of complaining, whining and self-pity in a supportive context is helpful here. There is a sense of humour here as well "poo explosions" which is able to keep perspective for the mothers as a group and It feels like a letting go of the small repeated frustrations that can occur when caring for a small child.

The qualities that make her friendship group supportive are described by Lynne-

> *There was just no judgment there, you know just really supportive the days where I would cancel last minute because I just couldn't even face going out of the house, um there was no …. oh gosh she's cancelling us again…. you know that sort of attitude* (Lynne).

The absolute acceptance and lack of judgment that she feels is innately supportive for Lynne. It is effective because it does not prevent her joining the group another day when she is feeling more

able to. It also returns to the concepts around acceptance and non-judgmental attitudes highlighted by Beth and Isla that are effective in terms of support because of their enabling quality that validates the mother's experiences. In essence the practical assistance with food provision or washing is similar. It validates the experiences of the mothers by accepting their struggle and need for support. However, in terms of coping, the mothers appreciate having a choice in the support that is given to them. Support that is implemented upon them does not engender feelings of being supported and can be experienced as undermining.

Effective support for the mothers falls into two main areas, emotional support and practical support. The emotional support is wide ranging and includes aspects such as; encouragement, thoughtfulness, checking in behaviours, feeling accepted and believed in, not feeling judged and a sense of emotional holding of difficult emotions. Practical support could be anything that supports day-to-day living; cooking, washing, shopping, cleaning, and supporting parental sleep deprivation. Sleep deprivation has been linked with depression as a causal factor in many studies (Karraker & Young, 2007; Rahamini, Rahamini, & Razaei, 2020; Titotzky, 2016; Wirz-Justice & Van der Hoofdakker, 1999). Supporting a mother's sleep deprivation has the potential to reduce the risk of depression in mothers and is an important dimension in the recognition of parental need for support in this area.

Family support has consistently been shown to be helpful to mothers living with mental health difficulties; with child-care, active listening and emotional support, and the provision of helpful information and advice being identified as being effective within a supportive context (Beard, 2019). Help with household chores and child-care has been found to be significant in helping mothers transition into motherhood (Leahy-Warren, McCarthy & Corcoran, 2011). Additionally close and caring relationships are linked to health and well-being through their ability to support in times of stress (Feeney & Collins, 2014; Leahy-Warren et al., 2011; Uchino, Bowen, Carlilse, & Birmingham, 2012).

Support is enabled by good relationships that can support through providing a safe environment and re-framing challenges into things that are more manageable problems. The experience of having positive attachment relationships particularly in childhood are found to influence how people respond to the social support that is offered to them. A study by Light et al. (2019) identified that mothers who had early experiences of trauma, reported their support networks to be less helpful and more upsetting and unpredictable than other mothers, leading them to seek support less often. Health and social care practitioners when supporting mothers who have experienced trauma or who have communicated poor relationships with attachment figures, need to be cognisant of this so that they can facilitate other avenues of support for these mothers.

Attending groups has been found to reduce parental anxiety as experiences and knowledge are shared and normalised with others who are experiencing similar things. However, for some mothers groups are not a place where they are able to relax or feel comfortable. The experience of effective support is very individual and assumptions about personal preference should not be made.

The dislike expressed by the mothers of 'unsolicited advice' is recognised. A study by Schaerer, Tost, Huang, Gino and Larrick (2018) with 290 participants found that women are more likely to receive unsolicited advice than men. They suggest that there is a power dynamic in advice giving in which the subtle interplay between power and advice can be a reason that unsolicited advice is so hard to bear. Another cross-cultural study by Chentsova-Dutton and Vaughn (2011), suggests that unsolicited advice can bear costs for the giver and the recipient, carrying a message that the recipient lacks important, skills, knowledge or competency.

There is a boundary between an individual's business and everyone's business and respect for individual's autonomy needs to demonstrate this. The mothers appreciate having a choice in the support that is given to them. Support that is given without the consent of the person to whom it is being given may be experienced as undermining whether it is verbal in terms of advice or practical help. Support is given within the context of relationships and if there is a lack of attunement within the relationship, the support may be targeted clumsily and lack effectiveness in supporting coping abilities.

In the next chapter we explore the mothers' experiences of asking for help, how it made them feel and how successful requesting help was for them.

Chapter Six

Being open and honest and asking for help

There are many reasons that can make it hard to ask for help. Having someone that you trust enough to ask for help is one, it can feel vulnerable. In terms of being able to ask for help over time, honesty and openness was perceived as really important by the mothers. However, it's difficult as it raises feelings of fearfulness and discomfort as Chloe here describes-

> *It is about being really brave and really honest in any way that you can, so like if you are not able to say that out loud, write it down, um and I think don't be afraid that people are going to judge you as a parent because of your mental health* (Chloe).

For Chloe it is a real indication of how hard it is for her, that she has developed a coping strategy of writing things down that she is unable to say out loud. She brings up the fear of being judged detrimentally as a parent because of her mental health, which could potentially be a reason not to be open and honest or seek help-

> *I think that that has always been a concern of mine that people will kind of listen to what I was feeling or thinking and go Huh! (Big intake of breath) This person shouldn't have children…. um and actually…. people kind of go…. oh you are dealing with all of that on top of having children, that's really tough….* (Chloe).

It appears to be deeply emotional for Chloe to talk about this. The pause that occurs in this extract for an audible breath prior to the expression of her fear of judgement, may bear witness to the fact that Chloe has thought this of herself at times. However, her experience in reality is more positive and she has found support and a sense of emotional attunement and positive regard, rather than negative judgments of her as a mother because of her mental health difficulties.

For Faye the process of reaching out is complex. She appears to be balancing her assessment of her current coping with her need to reach out-

> *So yes I am sort of questioning whether to or not at the moment I am just feeling not quite ready to reach out but um I might do.... I think we'll just see how long this goes on for and how well I'm coping* (Faye).

Faye is making an assessment of herself; of her current coping abilities and whether she is ready to reach out. It feels difficult for her to make a decision, this is a complex private decision that only she can make.

Beth describes a situation when she attended a pregnancy scan, where she was unable to be honest about how she was feeling, because of the totally opposite expectations and lack of congruence with her listeners-

> *I couldn't explain it to the midwives because they're all like.... well congratulations.... you know because everyone thinks it's wonderful news there's a baby on the scene but actually, they don't know anything that's gone on before and what I might be feeling otherwise* (Beth).

It is an understandable dilemma, which however leaves Beth with no opportunity to be open about how she is feeling and thereby also access support. Beth offers insight in to how she thinks about being open and honest about her feelings-

> *I think at your lowest point I think you are the least likely to reach out to someone, because it's at that moment that you feel like giving up and stopping, you're not looking at a lifeline then you are looking for someone to come and rescue you and then you're wallowing in the fact that no one's coming to rescue you but it's on the days where you feel a little bit better that you actually consider that things might actually be worth talking to someone about* (Beth).

At rock-bottom Beth is unable to see any value in reaching out for support, but when she is feeling a little better, she has some hope that there may be support available to her.

In her second interview Dawn discusses her continuing intrusive thoughts concerning her child's safety-

> *I still have a lot of anxiety about him um being involved in a car crash, choking, dying in his sleep I suppose the cot death thing is still really high up* (Dawn).

When questioned about how she is coping with these distressing thoughts, she pauses and then says that she is telling people more-

> *(sigh) um (pause) not much at the moment, um I'm telling people more* (Dawn).

There is again a sense that this is still not easy for her. There is a feeling of wanting to hide such thoughts away as if they are experienced as shameful. She clarifies later that "Saying it out loud to someone else" is helpful and makes a difference to her in terms of coping with the intrusive thoughts she is having. Having a meaningful connection with another person in some ways appears to reduce their significance and places things in a better context for her. She is also able to seek comfort and place her fears in a more normalised context, thereby reducing their impact.

Ellie finds that asking for help for a second time was not as difficult for her when she has to go back to her doctor-

> *Asking for help the second time and asking to speak about your medication a second time is a lot easier than the initial kind of…. yes I might need a bit of help here…. So I think coping wise…. knowing about it and knowing that you should really be able to do it yourself and you shouldn't feel bad for having to have things that help you cope* (Ellie).

She is more confident here in several ways: she is able to make the assessment that she does need help; she knows that she really wants to be able to do it on her own but that the medication will help her achieve this; and she understands that she doesn't need to feel bad about needing the help.

Ava specifically recognises being open and honest and able to ask for help as a coping mechanism for her-

> *Just being honest, being open and talking with everybody, I think that's positive in itself because you are not just hiding it away or keeping it*

*inside and letting things bottle up, so **I** think that for me has been a really good coping mechanism* (Ava).

The value for her is in not bottling things up inside herself or hiding the difficult feelings away. There is a feeling of discomfort and shame in the hiding and a feeling of release in the ability to reveal what she is feeling. Ava here clarifies the importance of self-honesty-

Just to talk and be honest with yourself and be honest with your closest people around you as well and ask for help (Ava).

The self-honesty is a pre-requisite of the ability to be honest with others. To be truthful with herself enables her to make more accurate assessments of her own needs and also then to communicate her needs. Ava is specific in her stipulation of the closest people around her to whom she can talk to. These are the people that she can trust the most and from whom she is able to ask for help.

In this theme there is a sense that being open and asking for help is difficult and can feel risky at times for these mothers. Asking for but not getting help could leave them worse off. It is difficult to be honest when there are feelings of shame and lack of self-worth being experienced. However, where they have had positive experiences of asking for help, it becomes a decision that is easier to make.

A US survey of 1400 women, found 40% of women with symptoms of mental and emotional distress did not seek help and consequently a significant proportion of Post Partum Depression (PPD) goes undiagnosed (Manso-Cordoba, Pickering, Ortega, Asunsolo, & Romeo, 2020). Fear of being judged is a recognised factor for parents not seeking help with children during a mental health crisis, particularly when speaking with support services where fear of losing custody is a concern (Khalifeh, Murgatroyd, Freeman, Johnson, & Killaspy, 2009).

Factors that can increase the likelihood of seeking support include having a previous mental illness and having other reasons to visit the GP (Khalifeh et al., 2009). Influencing factors for seeking support include levels of psychological distress, stigmatizing attitudes to mental health difficulties and perceived effectiveness of professional help available (Machi, Yamauchi, & Sugimari, 2016).

Ava's recognition of the importance of self-honesty is an obvious pre-requisite, if we can't be honest with ourselves, we will be unable to be honest with someone else. However, this is dependent upon individual defense mechanisms and coping styles, with avoidant styles potentially struggling more in this area. The reaching of rock-bottom, as Beth suggests may not be a time that enables help-seeking behaviours. Montgomery, Mossey, Bailey and Forchuk (2011) found that an intense experience at rock-bottom can jeopardize both the safety of the mother and the infant and that supportive measures need to be facilitated before this point is reached. For the mothers there is a journey towards help seeking behaviours that involves: self-awareness; being honest with themselves; and the ability to take a risk and trust in a positive response that can provide them with the support that they need to cope.

The next chapter looks at the sorts of experiences that we can really struggle to talk about, the things not spoken about by us or by our families or by society as a whole. We live in a fairy open age, but we still have areas where we find it difficult to be honest.

Chapter Seven

Things not spoken about

This theme connects with and builds on the previous theme of being open and honest and asking for help. The ability to be truthful with the self was found to enable a more accurate assessment of needs which can then lead to being able to communicate need. This theme contains some pivotal data in terms of the ability to seek help. There are things that the mothers for many different reasons struggle to speak about.

Isla described the difficult birth she had experienced with her child and her inability to tell anyone what she had experienced and how she was feeling-

> *I didn't tell them anything initially about things that I was struggling with* (Isla).

The reasons that it was so hard to talk about are complex and multi-faceted. One of the reasons was a sense of the absolute raw intimacy of the experience. Isla had not initially been able to process the experience enough to put it into words in a way that she was able to share with anybody. The experience is intimate to her vulnerable physical body and too personal to share lightly as she explains here-

> *It was humiliating, um becoming incredibly conscious that the entire world asks about your birth story, and thinking that's really personal, if I'd*

had an operation on anything else, nobody would say tell me everything about it, but because you've had a baby, every ones like go on go on tell us the whole story…. no that's really personal, we are dealing with a really intimate part of my body here, if I don't want to talk about it I don't have to (Isla).

Isla questions why it is expected that she should share such an experience. Is childbirth a public occurrence? Even then there is a realisation that 'the public' would only want a sanitised version of the real physical details, not the devastating distressing, disturbing and painful aspects that she had experienced. Isla then relates a more complicated feeling of shame that she failed at the perfect birth and shame that she is feeling bad because she has a healthy baby and has no right to feel bad-

> *Because it didn't go perfectly and that's what doesn't work in my brain, is feeling like that didn't go perfectly so that's…. I'm ashamed of that…. I'm ashamed that I didn't do it…. it's stupid because she's here and she's alive and she's in one piece so….* (Isla).

This complex mix of raw emotions of sadness and grief, the loss of the expected birth, feelings of shame bringing with it the idea that she could have done it better, even when it is clear that she absolutely did all that she could have done, and anyway it was outside of her control. The expectation of happiness at a healthy birth outcome in this case is denying Isla the ability to process her pain, her struggle and her sense of loss.

Jinny relates her difficulty in coming to terms with her experience of having depression and the relationship of this with the fact that it was something not spoken about-

I had post-natal depression, I've had it with all three of the children, but I didn't have any awareness of it before I had her, so it was quite.... I did find it quite difficult to get my head around (Jinny).

When asked about her understanding of the possibility of having mental health difficulties before having the children, she replies-

No none at all, it was never.... yes never spoken about in our family (Jinny).

Later Jinny describes a "hiding" away that has a feeling of the shame of the unacceptable, not spoken of, not presentable part of her existence-

I was very poorly, I had quite a lot of time just hiding at home and not wanting to do anything and just getting through the day (Jinny).

Jinny knew how poorly she was, but her only aim was to 'get through the day', an existence but not able to live a complete life. In terms of coping Jinny had previously had to resort to extreme measures to survive and to protect the safety of her children-

Something just came over me, it wasn't me at all and I was just.... I decided that I couldn't be a parent anymore, so I phoned (husband named) to come home and I packed a bag and I left.... I left (second child) with (first child) who were fifteen months and two week old, and I just.... ran away (Jinny).

This use of extreme avoidance may be socially unacceptable on some levels but is merciful and enables survival at the most critical of times. The consequences of the unspeakable for individuals can be the resultant unmanageability of things that can be frightening in consequence. She continues-

> *I was gone for three days with no contact, I just hid away in a hotel room in (town named) no idea why, but then on that third day I think hormones had started to settle a little bit so I phoned my GP and I said what had happened, made the appointment, came back, went to the appointment with him, got straight on to anti-depressants* (Jinny).

Jinny was able to use the time away to recover a sense of what she needed to do and was able to seek the appropriate help and support for her own sake and the sake of her children. The re-establishing of a sense of coherence here is palpable: my life is understandable; my life is meaningful; my life can be manageable if I access authentic care and treatment.

The mothers appear to recognise that certain aspects of themselves may be difficult for others to accommodate when they are expecting the new mum to be happy, positive and thankful. Beth previously has described the difficult emotions that emerged for her when she became a mother, "motherhood made me incredibly negative all of the time" and this resonates with Isla's difficulties with sharing the negative aspects of her experiences. The unspoken assumptions about what other people are able to listen to may be based in reality or not, but do make it hard to share negative emotions around the positive occurrence of a new baby.

For Chloe her diagnosis of ante-natal depression was something that she felt unable to talk about-

I was signed off work with ante-natal depression. Um so my pregnancy was really really tough, I…. so the trouble with ante-natal depression is you get signed off work for a period of time, and there is not really any dealing with it, I was told I could call 'Let's Talk', I didn't call them (laughs) um I wasn't really in kind of fit kind of mental state I didn't want to…. I was really embarrassed by feeling like that um my whole family were really really excited, so I didn't want to tell them that I was feeling like that (Chloe).

Her family is excited by the news of her pregnancy but Chloe is embarrassed by her depressive emotional state that she perceives as out of sync with the emotions of other people close to her. The contrast of these opposing emotions creates a barrier to her ability to share what she is going through.

Dawn experiences a resonating emotional reaction on the birth of her child-

I just looked at him and thought Oh my God, I've made a terrible, terrible mistake (Dawn).

When everyone is full of congratulations and happiness at the safe delivery of a new baby, it becomes hard then for mothers to share their feelings of doubt, dismay and fearfulness. The desire to fit in with the majority of emotions around you and be seen as good or even usual in this respect can potentially place pressure on mothers subliminally not to share their negative feelings about pregnancy or the new infant.

The aspects of coping behaviour can be in both the sharing and the withholding of negative emotions. The behavioural avoidance and mental withdrawal in the withholding of negative emotions may be a form of escape. However, it will not facilitate the appropriate attainment of support or comfort.

The things not spoken about for Dawn are the unacceptable face of motherhood-

> *I just want women to stop being told that they will feel this rush of love and you know when they first look at their child it's not always a rush of love, it might be a rush of.... what the 'f' have I done... which was my experience and I think that ahh it just needs to be more public, it needs to be said more.... It's hard it's really hard* (Dawn).

The need to speak about the variety of responses that women can have when they give birth is emphasised here. The feeling that Dawn expresses is one of exasperation that is based on the insight of her own experience, that she felt totally unprepared for, in terms of knowledge or in terms of emotional flexibility of how she could feel towards her child after giving birth.

The things are not spoken about for a variety of reasons. It is too intimate and too personal for Isla, or not spoken of in the participants family for Jinny. There appears to be a strong component of the subject matter being perceived as unacceptable to others. It is complex for the mothers, they are vulnerable and show the use of avoidant coping strategies in an attempt to protect the self from a more public sense of embarrassment, shame or blame and the potential for further distress and discomfort.

Avoidant coping strategies can be seen to have several aspects including a focus on emotional and behavioural detachment towards other people. However, although this is usually seen as unhelpful, it has been found that at times it can lower distress and support coping (Carver, Scheier, & Weintraub, 1989). Nevertheless, from the perspective of support seeking it can be disabling, as others are unable to offer care if the unspeakable remains unspoken. There is a link between more avoidant coping styles and low well-being, but this is found to be mitigated by social support in a study by Chao (2011). Carver et al. (1989) also suggest that social support can act as a bridge between more active planning styles of coping, emotion-based venting of emotions and avoidant styles.

The benefits of being able to be emotionally honest for an individual within a safe environment can include an increase in physical, mental and emotional well-being. This occurs through the enabling of the integration of trauma, which leads to more effectively implemented coping strategies. As we speak to another person about things that trouble us, we are able to make sense of what has happened. The confronting and making sense of our difficulties within conversation with a supportive person, can support us and enable the processing of difficulties and the planning of coping strategies (Snyder, 1999). Social support in this way can be central to our well-being. However, avoidant strategies can be understood in the context of attempts to protect the self from emotional pain and from the aspect of health care providers, it needs to be considered that a woman may not want to disclose the level of her depression to a health professional (Stone et al., 2018).

In the next chapter we consider a slightly nuanced aspect of self-honesty, the process of owning mental health. The owning of their mental health emerges as important for the mothers in terms of recognition, acceptance, accommodation, and adaptation. It is the ability to recognise how we are feeling, how we are behaving, or how we are coping and be honest with the self that comes before the ability to seek support.

Chapter Eight

Owning mental health

As we have seen there is a difficult process for the mothers in terms of recognising their own mental health needs and communicating these needs with others in order to seek support and appropriate help. The ability to recognise our own mental health needs precedes any other actions that we might need to take in order to look after ourselves. Kelly here explains some of the processes she went through before getting diagnosed with post-natal depression when her baby was 9 months old-

> *I'd had depression in the past, um but it really sort of snuck up on me I didn't actually recognise any of the signs at all* (Kelly).

The inability to recognise her own mental ill-health in some ways showing the daily struggle that she was just accepting. Kelly eventually gets to a point where she feels she just can't do it anymore and acts protectively of her infant and tells someone-

> *I did ring the health visitor, one day when the baby was just playing on the floor and I just said…. I just don't think I can look after him any more* (Kelly).

Kelly describes taking the standard Edinburgh Postnatal Depression Scale questionnaire used in the National Health Service (NHS) protocols which in this instance was unable to listen to her actual words and did not identify that she was significantly depressed and she had to struggle on, potentially putting both her and the baby at risk. She recounts-

> *Then a couple of weeks later, I just got really emotional and had sort of a huge argument with my husband um and I just felt like I was really acting out of character sort of like I left the house because I just needed to get away, um and I just said to my mum.... I'm just going to book myself in to the doctors, and I went to the doctors um and I think I started talking about it and I just kind of burst into tears and she pretty much sort of started writing me a prescription there and then* (Kelly).

The second experience is one of being heard. Kelly's recognition of her own need for support with her mental health and her bravery in seeking that support, demonstrates the real owning of her mental health needs. Lynne also describes a similar state of physical and emotional exhaustion and finding the limits of her coping-

> *Yes I think it just took all of my energy to look after them emotionally and physically because I was just so exhausted* (Lynne).

The reaching of the point of recognition for Lynne was influenced by her protective instincts towards her children. She describes reaching a low point and realising that her mood was affecting her children's behaviour-

> *When I was at my lowest um with my anxiety and depression I think more of that side of you comes out and your tolerance of things is a lot less um (pause) and then that kind of escalates their behaviour I think... so it was I think for me making that decision, to go back to the GP's and get my anti-depressants and stuff was the turning point* (Lynne).

The owning of and acknowledgment of her behaviour, becomes a critical point in the recognition of her own needs and her ability to seek help. With the protective instincts in her mothering role providing her motivation, she is able to set priorities and be flexible and realistic about what needs to be done. This problem-solving approach involves doing what works and doing it again, when necessary, even when it is not what you want.

Grace recounts a corresponding memory here, concerning the lack of recognition of her mental ill-health, and then a gradual acknowledgement, as things get worse for her-

> *But I didn't really realise it until I was kind of six months, maybe four to six months I think, post-partum, and I kind of started to say stuff to my husband that I think (child) should be happier.... I don't think I really wanted to kill myself, but I felt like I was the one upsetting her* (Grace).

This feeling that her child might be better off without her seems significant; it appears to be a warning sign and again the mother places her child's needs before her own as protective her instincts are deeply felt.

This awareness that things are not ok appears to be essential in the help seeking progression, and the owning of this knowledge to the point that it can be said out loud, is significant. Hazel puts it like this-

> *I think for me is that it's recognising that something's a problem or something is difficult and then trying to practically overcome it or address it in some ways* (Hazel).

This is self-reliant in nature and feels self-reflective, there is a 'recognition' of the problem or difficulty, and then the opening up resources to be considered. However, the coping options may not all be positive or protective of health and well-being, and therefore this may be a critical turning point for mothers. The surrounding support structures coming in to play in this pivotal moment.

Grace here describes how difficult it is to know what the helpful options are, as people try to make her give up breast feeding her child so she can get some rest-

> *I felt like everyone was just telling me that I should give her some formula and then you know…. you would get some sleep or you'd be better rested or somebody else could do it so that I could have a break but…. that actually the breast feeding was the main thing, and I always feel like it's always annoyed me, and it would still annoy me, that was the thing that was holding me together, because it was the only thing that she really needed, or it felt like she needed me for it…. Yes, I didn't want actually to give up the…. the thing that she needed from me…. do you know in that way…. The thing that only I could give her* (Grace).

This cry from the heart from Grace that breastfeeding was "the only thing that I could give her", so powerful in conveying that giving it up was not what she needed. What is unclear is consideration of all the practical things that could be given to attain more rest, such as cooking, cleaning, laundry, shopping for example, which may have been more helpful to her. Later Grace reflects on the times when she has been unwell-

> *I feel like I'm on the other side of it now, do you know and it feels like there is good days and bad days and my good days and bad days are more*

like everyone has probably, I think my mental health has improved quite
a lot so sometimes it's quite hard to think back and recognise how bad it
was at times do you know that way (Grace).

The awareness of lack of awareness, feels protective in some ways.
It is not denial because there is insight present, and it maybe helpful
to her ability to move on. However there remains an owning of her
mental health situation. Grace is able to reflect on her expectations
of herself with her first child-

I think with F (first child) I felt like I…. I had to get it exactly kind of
right and that was too much pressure (Grace).

The realisation that she was putting too much pressure on herself
is helpful with her subsequent child, in her appreciation of more
realistic expectations for herself as a mother. Grace is better able to
judge what is achievable with her second child. This is important in
terms of her mental and emotional well-being. In terms of coping,
it demonstrates an accommodation and acceptance, she is able to be
flexible, adjusting her preferences to her options. It shows her ability
to consider and take ownership of her own mental health.

Ava here describes her conscious awareness of her mood states, as
an important influence on her good or bad days-

I think it all depends on my mood for some reason, whether I've had a
rough night's sleep and am overtired, or now I'm back at work, if I've
had a difficult day at work, I've come home, I'm having to do tea, bath,
bed, um, so I think it all depends (Ava).

She is taking ownership of this in a helpful way. There is a sense of taking of responsibility. For Ava there is a necessity to as she says "be honest with yourself", that is enabling of the ability to get the appropriate help and support.

Chloe speaks about the difficulty she had recognising that her behaviour was of concern-

> *So when she was born and I was so in love with her um I didn't realise that a lot of my behaviour was actually not very normal* (Chloe).

This resonates as when we are going through something not experienced before, it can be difficult to differentiate what is healthy and what is not in terms of a new normal.

Faye is able to describe how she needs to listen to her own emotions and give them some space to be processed and managed-

> *If I'm feeling depressed I try and check in with that emotion, and actually like give that emotion some time and think right why am I feeling depressed? What's happened? Or if anything has happened, um where's this come from and that can just like.... um (pause) I think that that's just the biggest thing for me, just giving that emotion the time of day* (Faye).

This is an emotional skill that she has learnt and that she gives priority to in the self-management of her own mental and emotional health. Faye demonstrates an ability to be emotionally responsive to herself and give herself time to acknowledge her feelings and in the process recognise, accept, accommodate and adapt. It is truly self-caring and self-reliant in coping style and protective of her available resources.

The mothers talk about their difficulties recognising their mental ill-health. However when the mothers are able to recognise the significance of how they feel, they can move on to an ownership and acceptance which enables them to begin the process of taking back control in a way that supports their coping.

Chloe develops an acceptance towards her mental health difficulties and is able to acknowledge it-

> *I think a big part of it for me is learning to be accepting of the fact that this is probably something that is…. I'm going to have forever, it's going to be there, it might not always… it might not always be bad but it is something that doesn't just go away, it doesn't just fix itself and that is quite a big thing to come to terms with, whilst also not letting it define me* (Chloe).

She is attempting to balance her acceptance with not letting it define her, it is an element of self that she needs to be attentive to but it is not the sum of her as a person, her personality, her strengths, her gifts, her motherhood.

Beth talks of the importance of understanding the significance of her mental health which for her is an absolute necessity-

> *We just sometimes seem to forget that your mental health is incredibly important and it can be the choice like between life and death or completely suffering or not* (Beth).

There is no illusion here for Beth. It is a matter of life or death for her. This recognition allows for due consideration of what is required to maintain wellness and prevent illness.

Transition to parenthood can be a period of acute stress in which there are enormous levels of adaptation. It has been shown that adults who are able to think about their own thinking, who can develop good mentalization skills despite experiencing adverse life events may be more resilient (Berthelot et al., 2019). When the mothers can recognise the significance of how they feel, they can move on to an acceptance and this enables them to begin the process of taking back control. One of the pivotal factors for some of the mothers is the need to protect their child. This promotes an imperative to move into acceptance and planning of support seeking behaviours and self-care strategies.

In the next chapter we consider the ability to learn from experience and adversity. The mothers show how reflection upon experience is a coping skill in itself.

Chapter Nine

Learning through experience and adversity

The ability to learn from experience and adversity is documented within the mother's interviews. This theme specifically explores the mothers lived experience of *Learning through experience and adversity* and builds upon earlier themes. The mothers described their own experiences of adversity and the learning that it can bring and also the learning that people close to them offer.

Jinny remembers how when she was growing up things were so difficult for her own mother that she feels her mother was unable to form secure relationships with her children. Because of this experience, she herself takes extra care that she attends to the quality of relationships that she has with her own children-

> *She had such a tough time being poorly when we were younger, there are five of us, that she's missed that relationship building that I really take care of now with my children* (Jinny).

Kelly is able to learn from her own experiences of difficulties caring for her new-born baby-

> *It doesn't really matter if you don't achieve anything during the day your baby's is only like four weeks old kind of thing, you just need to be ok* (Kelly).

Kelly develops an acceptance of her own limitations here and this is for her a way of coping. She is able to restructures her experiences into understandable and thoughtful reflections.

Grace describes being influenced by her father in searching for the positives to look forward to-

> *I think my dad probably always did the finding something to look forward to thing* (Grace).

This interesting recognition of her father's influence examples a cross-generational transfer of resiliency and coping strategies. It is not possible to know how far back in the generations this strategy goes without speaking with Grace's father, but at some point, he has developed this strategy or has similarly inherited it. Grace is also able to identify her mother's influence of her in using the outside as a place that she is able "to clear my head" -

> *I think my mum probably always encouraged us to go outside, I've always found like if I'm out in nature that it will be.... easier* (Grace).

This trans-generational influence is being seen here again and shows the importance of the inter-generational passage of resilience and coping. In this passage Grace explains that her mother who died of cancer when Grace was 13 years old, was able to intentionally leave some letters of advice for her children before her death-

> *She had kind of left us all a couple of letters and that was her piece of advice to me was that um if you need help you have to keep asking for it and if you're not getting it from someone, you just have to ask the next person, and not be offended if somebody can't help you it's to do with them not you and just keep asking that's all* (Grace).

This ability to ask for help, and to keep asking, was a precious jewel that her mother was giving Grace, not to be ashamed for needing help, and to keep asking even if some people are unable to help. The ability to recognise that when other people are unable to help, it is to do with them not the help-seeker is insightful and enabling. Not taking it personally if someone is unable to help you can ease the way to asking someone else. The memory of the letter was precise and readily recalled. It had become part of Grace's coping repertoire.

Recognising the effectiveness of a coping strategy enables it to be used purposefully to facilitate coping. This recognition of coping strategies also enables the development of a coping repertoire that can be consciously accessed in times of need.

Hazel describes learning from her recognition of her child's needs, how to meet some of her own needs-

> *So I'm sort of recognising what she needs and applying it to myself to recognise what I need, so do I need some like quiet time or do I need ....*
> *am I tired, am I hungry, am I you know upset about something that's happened this morning is kind of like, trying to apply how I look after her to how I look after myself* (Hazel).

Hazel's mind-mindedness for her child, tuning into what her baby might be thinking, feeling or needing, has provided insight for herself in the recognition of her own legitimate needs. This recognition of the value of attending to her own needs can enhance her ability as a parent and is protective of her child. This form of coping is meeting her own needs through developing an attitude of self-compassion. It is also self-reliant and protective of her personal resources. Hazel is able to understand the potential loss of self that can come with meeting the needs of others to the neglect of self-

> *I can't put everybody else first before myself all the time because there will be nothing left of me* (Hazel).

It is not completely clear when this realisation happened for her, except that through her observations of her child's legitimate needs, she is able to experience and validate her own. Hazel also finds the acceptance of her own choice and responsibility in deciding to have a child helpful. It supports her resolve to be as good a parent as she can be. It is realistic and clear in its reasoning and that helps it become manageable. She says-

> *I mean we chose to have to have a baby so I guess that's oh I don't know if it's really hard.... um knowing that there's just me and (husband) to do it (laughs) it our response... you know it's our responsibility* (Hazel).

This acceptance of her ultimate responsibility in her own choices and for the care of her child is supporting of her coping resolve. Hazel is also able to imagine helping her child in the way that her child has enlightened her-

> *I think for me things that I want to pass on to her, it's sort of a bit of a circle, because the things that I want to pass on to her are the stuff that she's teaching me to do, (laughs) like to be.... sort of the stuff about being resilient that she is teaching me about myself that I hope that I can pass back to her, so we are sort of guiding each other in a way* (Hazel).

Hazel has developed a relationship with her child that enhances her coping and provides a sense of purpose for the future for them both.

The use of the word 'circle' provides an image of containment and of continuance in a sustained way as Hazel and her child cope together, as a coping dyad. Coping together in the intimate support relationship of mother and child together.

In this next passage Hazel remembers aspects of adversity from her childhood and reflects on her inability to express or talk about what was happening to her-

> *I don't think I ever talked about being bullied, I certainly didn't talk about my parents' separation, and so over the years I think I've probably internalised an awful lot of that and it kind of causes.... not causes me but it's fed into who I am and I think yes if people are going through something or feeling things it's important that they talk about it, even if it's to a parent or a friend, do you know what I mean, I'm not saying they have got to go and seek professional help, I just mean to vocalize what they are feeling so they can understand it better....* (Hazel).

Hazel concludes from her reflections that in the past she has been unable to talk about things, which if she had been able to talk them through, she would have been able to understand things better. The ability to process better her early traumatic experiences would have been beneficial for her. The ability to learn through experience and adversity can, in this way, develop coping resources for the future.

Beth has a large repertoire of coping strategies by the time of the interview when her child is eighteen months old. However initially she does not perceive these as coming from her experiences of adversity. When asked "what ways of coping came out of your past experience of coping with difficulties" she initially replies,

"Absolutely none, none no". However, at another point she can see a connection-

> *It was the dread from my own experience of being a child that drives me as well to be better* (Beth).

The ability to learn from negative as well as positive experience may have been surprising for her.

However, with Ava in this next passage, you get a sense that her developing confidence in her general ability to cope is more important than her learning through specific experiences-

> *I think being confident in your coping mechanisms of knowing what's best for you* (Ava).

In this "knowing", Ava communicates an awareness of her self-knowledge and that this is important and helpful for her.

Both mothers have undergone adversity in their early experiences of motherhood. Beth's experiences in some ways are more extreme and the help she receives from professional support services are more complex. It is interesting that Beth subsequently develops a large repertoire of coping skills of which she appears to be aware of.

The ability to reflect on the self is clear in Chloe's interview and it is this ability that presents learning opportunities for her. She is worried about the risk to her children of mental ill-health and adjusts her parenting style as a consequence-

> *I am really aware that children with parents with mental health conditions are more likely to have mental health conditions themselves so*

I'm really keen to do what I can to make that less likely. So in terms of my parenting style, we don't um…. we don't allow them to cry and I try to be really attentive towards them because leaving babies to cry is known to change their brain development (Chloe).

Chloe is thinking things through from her children's perspective and reflects further back to her own experiences of being parented and has makes conscious decisions about how she wants to parent her own children-

I'm very aware of what sorts of things were…. how things were dealt with when I was a child, and how they're not the way I want to do things with her (Chloe).

There is an absolute decision by Chloe that she wants to do things differently. The decision is made by reflecting upon her own experiences as a child. Chloe demonstrates an on-going ability to be reflective. She observes her child's self-talk one day and is concerned for her-

She has a rainbow toy which is sort of a stacker, it's um semi circles of wood and she placed it against her stomach and said 'I've got a big fat tummy just like mummy'. And I thought there's no way that she's…. she's got that from watching me getting dressed in the morning, that's the only place she could have got it from. And it made me realise that actually I need to be really careful about how I talk to myself, in front of her because I don't want her to do that (Chloe).

Chloe recognises the need to moderate her own behaviour so that her daughter does not copy her negative self-talk. Chloe's protective stance for her children and her ability to demonstrate reflective function are an instrumental part of her ability to learn from her experiences and from adversity.

Dawn's reflections in this passage are painfully honest as she realises what she viewed as a strength might not be-

> *I felt over the years that I was letting myself, where I thought I was being laid back in a relationships, I started to think maybe I was more of a walk over* (Dawn).

This recognition is empowering for Dawn. She is now equipped with knowledge that she can use to improve her life as an individual, as a partner and as a mother.

The learning that Ellie demonstrates from reflection is around her value as a mother-

> *I might not think that I'm good enough for them, but nobody else is going to be better* (Ellie).

Ellie has concerns about her abilities as a parent, but she knows on reflection that no one else would be able to take over and do a better job. This information is motivating for her and helps her to carry on when things are difficult for her.

Faye reflects on her experiences as a child of her mother's anxiety-

> *When I was a child she'd be like…. 'Oooh don't do that you are going to fall and hurt yourself' …. and things like that…. or 'don't do that because of this….' And you do pick up on things like that and then I was very anxious to do anything because I thought I was going to hurt myself*

and I didn't want to have new experiences because I was frightened so I definitely picked up on my mum's anxiety (Faye).

Faye is able to discern that she was influenced by the expressed anxiety of her mother. She understands the influence that it had for her in making her fearful of new experiences and she seeks to protect her child from this-

It's something that I'm trying not to project now on to my child (Faye).

Her ability to reflect on this experience from her own child's perspective, gives her the resolve to try and do things differently. In this way adverse experiences can be protective for future generations if there is the ability to learn from them. Faye describes her own character as a child-

I was quite shy, quite timid, and I always wanted to make everyone happy so if I drew a picture for my mum I'd have to go and then draw a picture for my Dad, I couldn't bear the thought that anyone would feel unequal um I probably wouldn't have given… if somebody had said…. what do you want to do today….. I would have been like whatever you want (Faye).

She recognises the inability of herself as a child to make decisions based on her own needs and when she watches her daughter develop confidence and independence, she is aware of her feelings about this-

It's nice when I see her go off and do something independently and not look back that gives me a sense of achievement as well that she's so secure and independent and happy that she feels that she can go and do that, so

it's a weird feeling because you want them to want you, but also you want
them to be, to be independent (Faye).

Faye is able to understand her ambivalence towards her daughter's
independence while really enjoying a sense that she has achieved
something as a parent, and that her daughter is developing in a
healthy way. This demonstrates coping in the form of emotional
intelligence, using self-awareness, self-regulation and relationship
management.

In this chapter the mothers demonstrate an ongoing ability to learn
from both past and present-day experiences in their own and their
children's lives. Experiences which are both adverse in nature and
positive in nature are used to inform and support their choices,
improving outcomes for them and their children. The experiences
are from childhood through to adulthood and also inter-generational
in nature. Having the ability to be reflective and examine lessons
learnt in term of coping is protective for individual mothers and for
their children.

Understanding the way that we can learn from adversity implies
that it can be a mistake to always attempt to protect people from
negative emotions. Maslow (1954, 2011) explains that "if grief and
pain are sometimes necessary for growth of the person, then we
must learn not to protect people from them automatically as if they
were always bad" (p.17). Maslow (1954, 2011) continues to argue
that the over-protecting from pain may imply a lack of respect for
the intrinsic integration of the person and their future development.
The ability to learn and grow from adverse experiences may be
able to be utilised in a significant way by mothers when caring for

117

their children. Certainly, the mothers in this study demonstrated protective instincts that were partly based on their own experiences of adversity.

This theme also relates to the previous theme's discussion of reflective functioning. The mothers describe experiences of learning and adaptation through their own experiences and the experiences of others including their own children. This is only possible through the ability to reflect thoughtfully on these experiences. Crittenden (2008) explains that when we reflect back on experience, we can integrate concrete and abstract information. This permits the integration of learnt knowledge in order that it can be applied to future experiences, and applying what we have learnt from past experiences to present or forthcoming circumstances, we can often be more effective in our actions.

Crittenden (2008) also discusses the most sophisticated form of reflective functioning. Metacognition which encompasses the ability to think about how the self thinks is exampled by Dawn when she realises the suffering she is causing herself because of her attitude to herself. Maslow (1954, 2011) states that "personal growth demands courage, self-confidence, even daring" (p.82). The mothers show their courage and daring in the face of adversity and their ability to grow through their experiences even when these are adverse.

Sometimes when we are dealing with adversity, *coping* can be asking for help. In the next chapter we will look further at what this can look like, the sources of support that can be accessed and where these can come from. Support can be interpersonal, relational, layered and multifaceted. In reality it is importance to have more than one source of help and support. Indeed, multiple layers are required by each of us in our everyday coping in life.

Chapter Ten

The importance of nested support structures

The concepts of layered or nested support structures were apparent in the mother's stories and the table below shows the wide sources of support that the mother's identified.

Support source	Ava	Beth	Chloe	Dawn	Ellie	Faye
Partner	✓	✓	✓		✓	✓
Family	✓	✓	✓	✓	✓	✓
Friends	✓	✓	✓	✓	✓	✓
Groups	✓	✓			✓	✓
Professionals	✓		✓		✓	
Work	✓					
Society						
Other	Social media Groups	Child's Nursery Nature	Nature	Childcare Cleaner Exercise and yoga	Child's school	Nature Exercise And yoga

Support source	Grace	Hazel	Isla	Jinny	Kelly	Lynne
Partner	✓	✓	✓	✓	✓	✓
Family	✓	✓	✓	✓	✓	✓
Friends	✓	✓	✓	✓	✓	✓
Groups	✓	✓		✓	✓	✓
Professionals	✓	✓	✓	✓	✓	
Work	✓				✓	
Society	✓					
Other	Landscape and environment	Being outside in nature	Social Media apps	Child's nursery	Child's nursery	Facebook Groups, Virtual Zoom Groups.

The mothers all spoke of their support structures in relation to their coping abilities. The significance of effective partner support cannot be underestimated when women are at their most vulnerable, coping with mental health difficulties and caring for a new baby. Isla describes the way her husband was able to support her emotionally and psychologically by challenging her negative self-talk-

> *I've definitely done a lot of beating myself up that I'm not good enough, that she deserves a better mum, um my husband's very good at challenging me on that and saying. . . . 'well go on tell me something that you've done today that's really awful, that ruined her life, that made her unhappy?' You know reminding me that actually he thinks that I'm brilliant and that (child) thinks I'm brilliant and so I think I'm starting to see myself more positively* (Isla).

The value of this intimate partner support is so significant because he is the one who is present with her and that actually knows what is going on for her. The giving of this positive feedback to Isla in her moments of self-doubt, helps her to restructure her view of her situation and the care that she is able to provide to her baby in a more positive light. This then enables her to carry on and be a more confident mother. The adaptation to motherhood is a complex and demanding process which can need this intimate level of support. The ability of an intimate support individual to notice that something is different with the mother in her personhood and that they are not like their normal self, is valuable and significant in terms of the consequent opportunity to offer care or support. Hazel explains this-

> *I think my husband was quite worried in the beginning um just because*

there were lots of tears with all the hormones and everything, that first couple of weeks were really hard (Hazel).

This picking up of the emotional clues by Hazel's husband led to help-seeking behaviour that eventually led to appropriate professional help.

Lynne is aware of having a 'support network' and gives an example of how the practical support was invaluable to her-

> *I've got quite a good support network around me I think that's been the major thing I think particularly in those early days with (first child) I just remember ringing my mum and saying…. I can't do it any more…. You know and she raced back from work, thankfully she could, took her out for a walk so that I could just have half an hour quiet* (Lynne).

The timely and responsive support given by Lynne's mother is restorative for Lynne's coping abilities. She is able to take some time for her-self, to strengthen and recover.

Grace is also aware of her support circle that includes her husband, her father, baby groups, friends - inner and outer circles, extended family, work, the landscape and environment and professionals such as the GP and health visitor. She says about baby groups that at the time she did not realise that they were a part of her coping-

> *I don't think I thought the baby groups were a coping skill, I think at the time I felt like um I should bring her to make sure that she had the right things for her development, put it that way, like I felt that it was about her, but I think looking back now I think it was about me coping (laughs) rather than about her doing all these great things do you know that she could do (laughs)* (Grace).

Grace recognises here in retrospect the value that attending the baby groups had for her in terms of coping. It allowed her to develop friendship groups and close friends whom she could turn to for support. Isla also talks about the support that she was able to access through attending a baby group. She describes how when she eventually was able to share some of her traumatic birth experiences with the mothers in the group, it was helpful not only to her, but gave permission to other mothers in the group to open up about their experiences-

> *I told them the story and I tried to make it relatively lighthearted, in the sense of, I'm ok.... I'm ok now um but this is what happened and this is how I felt um and it was amazing because they were all brilliantly supportive, which I knew they would be, but also it made some of them open up* (Isla).

Isla is protective towards the other mothers in the group and tries to sanitise her description of her traumatic birth experiences so that she does not frighten the other mothers. She expresses amazement at the level of support that the mothers were able to give her following her opening up about her experiences. The sharing of difficult experiences surrounding the births of the other mothers then becomes possible for the group. There develops an ability for real practical support within the group-

> *One of the girls the other day was like.... I really feel I can't cope because my house is always a mess and I'm used to it being tidy and I can't do anything because I'm always worried about the hoovering.... And um I said, alright I'll bring (child) over and I'll watch yours, you do your hoovering, and it was like, we'll have a little cleaning play date and in return you can come to me and I'll do mine....* (Isla).

123

This "cleaning play date" is incredibly supporting and enabling; the practical problem-solving supporting successful coping, emotional balance and mental well-being.

The picture diversifies somewhat with the outer layers of the support systems, with two mothers feeling supported by their workplace. Kelly relates how the Human Resources (HR) Department in her workplace supported her-

> *It's quite a big company we've got a well established HR um I got support before I left about how to go about preparing for maternity leave and preparing to come back from maternity leave with …. keeping in touch days…. and things um and actually they were very good when I got the post-natal depression* (Kelly).

Kelly feels supported by them as she prepares to go on maternity leave and also later in her return to work. She points out that she worked for a larger company with an HR department on site, the implication being that this may not be the case with smaller less established workplaces.

Only one mother discussed support from the state or society. She lived in a part of the country that provided the "baby box" scheme; these boxes' contain essential items for the baby and the funding is by regional government-

> *It's not like we couldn't have afforded all the things that …. just all the things that were in it that were all perfectly designed for do you know you just wouldn't have picked the right things almost, and we still use the actual box as a toy box (laughs) it's so good* (Grace).

It feels as if Grace valued the well-chosen contents of the box and in turn this helps her feel valued herself in some way.

Two mothers felt significantly supported by their childcare providers who supported their return to work. The participants also discuss several sources of social media-based support, in particular friendship groups which were used as a communication strategy. This may potentially have been enhanced by the needs of social isolation in the Covid-19 lock downs in 2020.

Dawn describes experiencing mixed levels of support from her partner-

> *My husband had two weeks off paternity, he slept for most of it and would go out to the gym, um they just have no idea, there should be some serious workshops out there for men, for partners* (Dawn).

His lack of understanding of her needs eventually contributes to her level of distress as she describes in devastating terms later "It broke me". Later the parenting does become more of a shared matter, and Dawn is able to appreciate this as supportive-

> *My husband took (child) to a farm where they picked apples and there was Shetland ponies and ducks* (Dawn).

However the biggest support source for Dawn together with her ability to return to the workplace, is exercise and yoga-

> *The gym had been such a pivotal point in getting out of my depression or at least um you know helping with the suicidal thoughts you know* (Dawn).

This she mentions above all else, for her as the thing that is her critical source of support-

> *I found a little corner downstairs in my work building (details omitted) and I roll out my er my yoga mat and work out there so during my lunch hour* (Dawn).

This form of support is inter-personal, and might be excluded from many concepts of support, but to Dawn it is a self-reliant form of support that she is in control of and is integral to her coping abilities.

Dawn contrasts the support she understands as expected for her husband's knee surgery and the support that she feels new mothers can expect-

> *My husband had a knee operation last year and he was fine, a little key hole thing and for six weeks he was recovering and now it's a big thing and it was all intense and I was looking after him and it was just a small cartilage thing and you just think there is so much you know after care done for that you know there is just not enough done for women after they... you know there is the oestrogen, the progesterone, the hormones, flooding, you know your body's going into shock, it might be caesareans, stitches* (Dawn).

The expectations around the accepted levels of support following child-birth for Dawn are experienced in contrast to the support that was recommended following her husband's knee surgery. She questions the acceptance that she perceives of society as a whole as to whether the support directed towards new mothers is adequate.

It is interesting that what Dawn lacks in the form of intimate partner support, she is able to take control of and make up for through her work, childcare, cleaner and the use of exercise. Her coping is interwoven with her environmental influences. In her own way Dawn has created nested support structures that can hold her in balance. The sources of support are strategically personalized to meet the needs of herself as an individual.

In contrast Faye emphasises the need she recognises to make connections-

> *After birth.... I think people is the biggest thing, is what I'm trying to get at.... connections and feeling like you are not the only person in the world that's staying up all night or um I think that's the biggest thing* (Faye).

Connecting with other mothers is important for her as it relieves the sense of isolation, especially at times when no one is around to help as in the middle of the night.
Similarly knowing that you are not the only one in this situation for Faye is what is effective-

> *When you can relate to other people it makes it a bit easier to talk about it as well, with other people as everyone feels anxious and down* (Faye).

The ability to share experiences with others is what is supportive for her. The school that her daughter attended was a source of support for Ellie-

> *I would call the school quite a lot in the first like two weeks that they went back and they were so brilliant.... and they'd say.... Yes she's fine she doing this.... so that helped* (Ellie).

Ellie was able to access support from the school that was supportive and enabled her to manage her levels of anxiety.

The nested structures of support can give firm and comprehensive care to mothers, but not all mothers are able to access these. Bronfenbrenner's (1979) ecological systems theory suggests areas of support including social connectivity and environmental factors. The mothers show their ability to seek support from intimate and wider sources creating the structure of nested support that can provide more of a safety net in terms of effective support, rather than relying on only one or two sources.

This theme was able to illuminate the mother's awareness of many of the external structures such as partner and close family support, community and professionals and extends the theme *Identifying effective support*. Leahy-Warren et al. (2011) in a study with 477 first-time mothers found that most frequently identified sources of support were mothers, husbands/partners and sisters. There has been a recognition of the value of support from partners or close family members, across several themes. These close relationships consist of the people that have that intimate knowledge about what is going on for the person and the ability to recognise when things are not working in a way that is safe or productive.

Levine and Kline (2007) describe internal support structures that include our personality strengths, such as initiative, ingenuity, intelligence and wisdom: and external support structures for example, supportive relationships, environments and community. The mothers are aware of developing as people as Beth describes in the theme *Learning the importance of self-care* "I'm developing as a human, and my highest level I have ever done". These internal resources are an aspect of nested support structures which are not always recognised.

Additionally, Leahy-Warren et al. (2011) found that lower levels of support were significantly linked with higher levels of depressions. Mothers with two children have been found to have higher social capitol, possibly through increased social opportunities from two children and increased need for reciprocity activities, such as child minding (Strange et al., 2015). Social capital can be thought of as the ability to obtain resources and support from our personal connections. There is an importance of sources of support that can promote resilience across individual; family; community; institutions; and culture.

The final source that Bronfenbrenner (1979) mentions is chrono-systems, which are time based. There are numerous examples from the mothers of time-based supportive influences from the cognitive aspect of being able to wait and endure until things get better, to the learning from experience over time. These are specifically included under other themes of *Mother's lived experience of coping* and *Learning through experience and adversity*. The ability to seek support from intimate and wider sources rather than relying on only one or two sources, creates the structure of nested support which provides a safety net that is better able to support coping. The additional temporal or time-based aspects of support structures and internal systems adds new dimensions to considering what can support coping in mother's who have mental ill-health.

In the next chapter the mothers discuss another source of support that was not included in this theme but emerged as an untold aspect of parenthood, the support that they perceive from their children in terms of feeling motivated, or inspired by them.

Chapter Eleven

Children as motivators

This theme *Children as motivators* was a part of 'coping' that the mothers identified where they talk about how the children inspire their coping in a variety of different ways. The mothers talked about experiencing a lack of appreciation and recognition for motherhood. However, they were able to feel inspired by their children in terms of the children's continuing development and the expressions of love that their children give back to them. Ava describes in this passage the love that her child expresses for her-

> *You just get so much back from them like he tells me he loves me and he gives me hugs just randomly and that just brings out so much* (Ava).

Ava is able to appreciate the love and affection that her son shows her. Ava explains that it brings out "so much", giving a sense that this can enhance her coping abilities as she is supported by her child's show of affection.

Lynne's description here resonates with Ava's in the appreciation of the love that she feels from her children-

> *Just those little moments of when they reach up and touch your face and things like that yes it's just um its lovely and I, the three of them now will just come up and hug me and go…. love you mummy…. And that just means everything to me really…. (laughs)* (Lynne).

The use of the word 'everything' here denotes the importance it has for her. There is a sense of the value that the loving actions of her children engender for her is inspiring for her as a parent.

For Ellie being able to enjoy her children makes up for the lack of any verbal appreciation from her wider social context-

> *It's little things like we will be going down the garden and they will suddenly stop and be really fascinated with a leaf because it's a different colour and I think as adults you lose that magic* (Ellie).

Her children are reminding her of the benefits of being mindful; being able to live in that specific moment, away from worries about the past or the future, and able to appreciate something as small as a leaf. There is also an understanding of being needed by her children for Ellie-

> *I might not think that I'm good enough for them, but nobody else is going to be better, so it's.... and like I know them so well.... I know when it's going to turn into a paddy, when one's going to start crying and you know it's a case of.... (child named) is quite sensitive she'll cry over pretty much anything and where as I will sit there and try and find out what's wrong and try and talk it out, a lot of people would be..... well right now (child named) that's enough now that's silly.... And like that doesn't help her* (Ellie).

Ellie is aware that she alone has the intimate knowledge and experience of what her children need. She recognises that even though she doubts her own value at times. She has a unique contribution to make and in this way she is needed. This signifies that she has a valuable contribution to make and in this way is motivational to Ellie as a mother.

Similarly, Dawn uses her knowledge of her son's needs to guide her parenting-

> *He likes to take his time in the morning so rather than scooping him out of bed and then stuffing him into some clothes you know he's a lot happier you know I've got time to see to his toddler needs really (Dawn).*

This responsiveness to her child's needs makes both their lives easier and more pleasant. She is allowing him to inform her parenting and to motivate her actions as a mother.

Faye describes trying to get her child to sleep and not knowing what to do next, when her child's smile lifts her from her state of being into an easier one, where she is able to carry on-

> *(child named) is helping me although it is hard and you know like when she is really, really excited, to go to sleep and I'm stood there rocking her and thinking…. oh my gosh what am I going to do…. But then she'll turn around and smile and that's enough sometimes just to get through (Faye).*

There is a sense of emotional regulation, a co-regulation between child and mother as her child smiles. Faye is helped by the smile and eye contact to feel calm, nurtured and safe and to have a sense that she can manage her child's needs in that moment. Later Faye describes how her child is able to live in the moment-

> *She can go from being the most upset about something you know falling*

over she is so upset, and she will go from that to just laughing and forgetting about it and doing something else and I think there is a lot to learn from that, she doesn't hold on to anything, she just lives completely in the moment, um whether that's being happy or sad, or angry or frustrated, she expresses that emotion and then moves on (Faye).

The ability of her child to express emotion relevant to the exact moment and then move on being unaffected by the recent past event and not holding on to any negativity is inspiring for Faye. She recognises that there are lessons to be learnt from her child in this respect. Her child is able to live mindfully in the present, in a way that can be hard for adults to do. Her child is not spending time worrying about the past or being anxious about the future and Faye recognises that she can learn from this herself.

For Ellie it is the requirement of the daily parenting tasks that are helpful to her-

I think because when you've got kids you can't just sit on the sofa, they have got to be fed, they've got to have their nappy changed, they've got to be given drinks you know you, I think that knowing that you have to get through the day gets me through the day (Ellie).

Ellie is aware of her practical responsibilities for her children. These have a rhythm and necessity which she finds enabling. She knows what each day will require of her, in this way there is a feeling of acceptance for her. She is able to accommodate all these practical aspects into her thinking and doing and demonstrates her abilities to adapt within her coping styles.

Hazel reflects on her parenting journey with her daughter-

> *I realised that you can read as many books as you like or you can speak to as many people as you like about what being a mum is about um but I kind of just let (child named) teach me in the end.... about it.... how to become a mum you know* (Hazel).

For Hazel the most important source of learning is from her own child. The becoming a mother is a joint endeavour with her daughter, finding out what works or what doesn't on a day-to-day basis.

Isla is captivated by her daughter and there is a sense of intimate engagement-

> *She's mesmerized by her own hands (laughs) everything is interesting, everything is new, we've started trying her on a few different foods um she's just fascinating, completely fascinating, I can't wait to see what she becomes when she's older and what interests her what makes her happy, what annoys her, all of the little things about her* (Isla).

The use of the word 'fascinating' twice in this passage suggests the strength of interest and attention that her daughter inspires in her. It is an expression of Isla's attachment and love for her daughter that in some ways is able to create this level of intense emotional focus. This focus can support Isla as a parent, helping her to be attentive and mindful towards her child.

Jinny similarly describes how she loves spending time with her children as she can see their personalities developing-

When they start to develop their personalities, so when they are coming up to that seven- or eight-month mark, I do love that age and love spending time with them (Jinny).

Her child's developing personality becomes important to Jinny as she finds it more interesting to spend time with them.

Kelly identifies her excitement in following her children's development-

Actually every stage along the way I've kind of been more excited about what they can do next kind of thing so.... (Kelly).

This focus is described as 'exciting' for her and able to inspire her enthusiasm in a positive sense.

The mothers are able to be inspired by their children's developing personalities, which feeds into their parenting understanding. There is a sense of mother and child learning together as a dyad, able to support each other in some ways through their joint experiences. The fact that they are the one that is best able to understand the intimate needs of their individual children appears to be able to help the mothers value their contribution. There is also an imperative to cope because the children have needs that have "got" to be met. These practical responsibilities have a rhythm and necessity, which can be enabling to coping. The element of feeling needed helps the mothers carry on. They have a sense that what they are able to do for their children is important and valuable. This helps them when they are not feeling their best or when they are doubting their mothering abilities; it binds them to a higher purpose.

During positive social interactions involving behavioural synchrony such as a shared gaze or touch, there has been found to be a physical hormonal attunement, involving heart rate and brain EEG patterns which can provide positive experiences and promote resilience (Morris, Hays-Grudo, Kerr & Beasley, 2021). Ensor and Hughes (2008) found that what mattered for children's social understanding was the 'meeting of the minds' within conversation, where shared mental states promote children's ability to understand others.

Some of the mothers describe finding the ability of their children to live in the moment inspiring, the interest in the colour of a leaf or the ability to not hold on to sadness and be happy in the moment. Smith (2010, p.365) describes it as "Zen-like" when a child notices beauty in the ordinary and points to Stadlen (2004, p. 89) when she says that a mother must "loosen her active conscious mode and sink into something older and simpler in order to get close to the world of her baby". The mothers have a joy and fascination in their children that supports their parenting. In the next chapter we look at how the mothers are able to pass on *coping* to their children.

Chapter Twelve

Passing on coping

All the mothers were able to articulate in terms of coping and resilience, what they wanted to pass on to their children. This presents as a protective factor within their parenting. The desire to help their own children to develop abilities and strategies that will help them cope in their own lives is apparent. Ava stresses the importance for her child of being able to ask for help and that it is fundamentally acceptable to need help sometimes-

> *But definitely I would like to pass on to M that it's ok not to be ok, if there is any point that you need something, or need some help, it's ok* (Ava).

It could be interpreted from this that this is something that Ava is able to accept for herself in her own life, or at least places enough value on to want to pass it on.

Chloe expands on this and introduces concepts around emotional competence; the ability to identify emotions and having the emotional confidence in being able to communicate them-

> *I think I just want them to be able to talk to someone when they need to, when it's important and about whatever they need to talk about and not have any fear with that and I think that that's about them having confidence in their own thoughts and feelings, and that's what I would like them to be able to do* (Chloe).

There is a tacit knowledge in this extract from Chloe about what it is like not to have confidence in your own thoughts and feelings. Chloe does not want this for her children; she wants them to be able to communicate their feelings without 'fear'. This implies that for Chloe herself, communicating your feelings can be fearful.

In this next extract Beth specifically points to her desire for her child to be able manage emotions. She relates this to her own life experience, where she did not have anyone to help her in this way, seeking for her child what she did not have herself. Beth feels that there is something lacking in her own personality which dates back to her childhood when she had no supportive adult that was able to help her manage her own emotions-

> *I don't want to discipline her for being angry, you know how some people do they're like 'stop crying, why are you crying!' you know it's like actually just recognise that they're upset and just be there for them and be like 'oh I see that you are upset, what's upsetting you' or 'it's ok you can cry, it's ok', because I don't know if I got that as a kid and that might have been a key part of my development that's missing and why I act the way I do, is because I lack that part of my emotional intelligence because I never had anyone to tell me how to do it because my situation as a child was difficult* (Beth).

Beth demonstrates her acquired knowledge of how she hopes to help her own child. She is able to break down the aspects that she feels can support her child's understanding: recognition of distress; acceptance of feelings; identification of emotions; and showing attentiveness to the hurt. For Beth being able to view something from the needs of a child, communicates value to her as an adult about what is necessary for a healthy emotional life for all people.

Dawn similarly seeks to help her child to be able to recognise when the emotions are his own, and to be able to be strong and sensitive to others without taking on other people's emotions-

> *I want him to erm to know that he is not responsible for other people's emotions, um I want him to stand strong and have his space in the world, um to be sensitive but be um (pause) not let people walk over him really to um yes be strong and fair* (Dawn).

Dawn explains that this is something that has affected her in her life; she has felt burdened by other people's emotions-

> *I absorb other people's emotions too much and um I don't want (child named) doing that, I want him to be supportive, but he doesn't have to take them on, they don't need to weigh down on his shoulders* (Dawn).

This is a complex issue that Dawn is exploring. Her insight into this emotionally protective stance has come from difficulties that she has gone through herself. To be able to maintain the ability to be supportive of others, whilst understanding safe emotional boundaries for the self, is insightful reflection on Dawn's behalf. It communicates a painful learning from adversity for her as she endeavours to pass on to her son this learned knowledge, in order to protect him from the emotional pain that she has experienced.

Ellie recalls her own mother helping her to calm down-

> *My mum was always really good at like coming down to my level, and going 'big breath, calm down, let me know what's wrong'* (Ellie).

This simple phase includes so much: the getting down on the same level indicating the giving of attention and the ability to listen; the instruction to take a breath engaging the calming systems of the body; and the last request to "let me know what's wrong" giving permission and space to share the reason for distress. The fact that Ellie can give this memory word for word, shows the significant impact that the approach had for her and is clearly valued and transferred from one generation to another in this way.

Faye includes in this extract concepts around validation of her child's emotional responses. In a similar way to Dawn and Beth, she draws on her own adverse experiences from childhood and wants better experiences for her own child-

> *I just want her to be confident in herself, every part of herself, um and to know her own worth um* (Faye).

When asked if that was something she felt that she didn't know and how this can be done, she replies-

> *No, definitely not… Validating her emotionally, physically, yes you know all we can do is our best* (Faye).

Faye is clear on how she wants to help her child feel validated and confident in her own worth. The importance of only being able do your best and no more is protective against unrealistic demands and expectations from self and others.

The developed insights of these mothers demonstrate reflective ability and protective capacities and show why mother's experiences of adversity can be built on positively to support them and their children. It is also apparent that when the mothers reflect upon the emotional needs of their children, it can support their insights into their own emotional needs and potentially lead to resilience building capacities.

The mothers are also able to clearly identify what it is in regard to coping and resilience they would like to be able to pass on to their children. Hazel can imagine helping her child in the way that her child has enlightened her-

> *I think for me things that I want to pass on to her, it's sort of a bit of a circle, because the things that I want to pass on to her are the stuff that she's teaching me to do, (laughs) like to be sort of the stuff about being resilient that she teaching me about myself that I hope that I can pass back to her, so we are sort of guiding each other in a way* (Hazel).

This resonates with Beth's experience of being able to view something from the perspective of the needs of a child, which is then able to communicate its value to her as an adult. Hazel has developed a relationship with her child that enhances her own coping and provides a sense of purpose for the future for them both.

For Isla, the concept that she wants to pass on can be interpreted as 'hope'-

> *That you can! Just that you can! You can always cope, you can always find a way, and whatever that is that works for her, her Dad and I will always be there, to help her with it* (Isla).

This assurance that there are solutions to be found and nothing is insurmountable in terms of coping appears to be Isla's message for

her daughter. This is placed along side and together with, the vow of available support. There is a sense of coming from a supportive place, a place where people will believe in you and your abilities. It is help seeking in reverse and the assurance of availability of support. There is acknowledgement of individual solutions, but emphasis is on the belief that solutions can be found. Hopefulness as a coping skill can be considered valid in this context, with the encouragement it engenders to keep looking for solutions to difficulties. It can be regarded as part of the family of emotional coping strategies. However potentially it could be avoidant in style as it incorporates wishful thinking and assumes that a solution can be found to every situation. It is also possible that it could be an inter-generational factor in terms of the parental influence in character or personality formation of the children.

Jinny similarly echo's this message of available support-

> *I would love them to know that its ok to not feel 100 percent all of the time, and that they've always got…. I want them to be able to come to me and (partner named) for support which I haven't been able to do with my parents* (Jinny).

It is for Jinny the experience of lacking support that she herself has had, which makes her value the importance of it as a coping strategy. She also wants her children to know that they do not need to be in top form all the time. In some ways this is an interesting acknowledgement of the existence of negative emotions that can be admitted and do not need to be denied. It might be cognitive in its reasoning and its approach to reality, but is possibly an emotional coping skill in its core essence. Jinny is saying that she and her husband are able to bear the difficult emotions as well as the happy emotions. This is enabling in that if she is successful in helping her children understand this, they should be able to go to her when they are not feeling ok.

Grace describes how her and her husband are trying to build in support for her children in terms of the ability to emotionally regulate which is a self-reliant coping skill-

> *We give them lots of cuddles and er we've built…. not built but created a little corner of the room with like cushions which has just all the books in it, so they will quite often say that they want to go in there, like a quiet corner um I think we've always done it "do you want to read a book?" so they will both quite often bring us a book, if they are upset and want to read a book so I think that obviously we've tried to instil in them a bit of quiet time to kind of calm down* (Grace).

Grace's acknowledgement of her children's needs for cuddles here, indicates her understanding of the need of her children for co-regulation in times of intense emotion. This potentially demonstrates a passing on to the children of learned pathways for self-regulatory skills. The making of a safe calm physical place for the children to be able to be in, with calming activities in the reading of the books, is transferring tools of coping that can be used in the long term and shows a pathway of inter-generational transfer of coping and resilience. It is self-reliant in nature and it is worth noting that a created calm space for the children could be replicated for the adults as well. There is an inference that reading is found to be calming for Grace herself.

The ability to be able to understand and express emotions is for Lynne what she is trying to give her children-

I can remember right from when they were babies, you know like if they were crying I'd try to kind of acknowledge it and say …. 'I know you're upset…' you know or if they are angry…. 'I know you are angry at that….' but or …. 'I know you are frustrated….' or…. 'Oh that's made you really happy hasn't it….' so they've always been able to um even right from when they were two and talking they have always been able to verbalize that (Lynne).

Lynne is acknowledging her understanding that having an emotional vocabulary, and to be able to accurately identify emotions from a young age, is part of emotional intelligence and that this is significantly connected with coping and resilient behaviours. Lynne has been labelling emotions for her children and helping them to match the emotion with the appropriate vocabulary. This ability to verbalize strong emotions is seen by Lynne as a positive self-reliant coping skill.

A skill that Kelly has learned her-self is also what she would like to pass on to her children-

That sort of like stopping and pausing and thinking you know, is everything all going wrong, or can you just make a quick change um I guess to have that kind of strength within themselves really (Kelly).

Creating a pause, a time to think, to reflect and consider options is a response approach which is the opposite to reactivity. It is essentially problem solving in its nature with the added emotional element of the internal 'strength within'. It feels positive too, a real strategic approach which could be transferred to many differing situations and difficulties.

The range of coping skills and strategies that the mothers are trying to pass on to their children is intrinsically linked to their own skills and abilities. What they themselves have found to be effective they feel confident to pass on to their children in a pro-active protective parenting attempt to teach their children to cope with adversity. The mothers show reflective capacity as they consider aspects of coping that they lacked and why it is important for their children to be able to have skills that they themselves were not given or did not have. There is a strong focus on helping their children to manage distress. Instinctively the mothers appear to recognise that resilience requires skills in coping with distress. There appears to be a tacit knowledge that the way that they manage distress in their children in childhood, will impact their children's lifelong skills of managing distress.

Reyes and Constantino (2016) propose that the transmission of resilience occurs by the observation of adults coping with the things that cause us stress, by children who then go on to have a coping repertoire to help them deal with stressors in their futures. Thus, creating resilience as an enduring phenomenon. Through this process resilience itself is conceptualized as a coping strategy. The mothers use their experiences to inform their behaviour with their children, knowing what they lacked, knowing what life's challenges can bring, knowing about what coping means to them as individuals. This strong protective stance of the mothers really comes through as they demonstrate practical steps that they take to provide their children with coping strategies and pass on resilience to them in this way.

Some of the mothers talked about reflecting back and considering aspects of coping that they had lacked and why it was important for their children to be able to have skills that they themselves did not. It was the awareness of lacking essential coping skills to cope with adversity that inspired them to help their children develop skills that they themselves had lacked.

Hazel points to a sense of a circle of learning as mother teaches the child, and child informs the mother about what her needs are. Crittenden (2008, p.339) explains that "healing comes one person at a time as a gift from a person who cares compassionately about another", and it involves "imagining a different future". The mothers seem to imagine a better way for their children and demonstrate protective reflective functioning. This is a critical entry point for supportive services to be aware of and can be used as a motivational aspect in family support interventions. However, Crittenden (2008) offers a note of caution, in that parents need to be seen as individuals in their own right and not solely in terms ability to fulfil their children's needs.

All the mothers in this study had partners, in the next chapter we look at the role of partners, examining aspects of intimate partner support and the ability of the relationship between parents to provide support for parenting within the family and for mothers' mental health.

Chapter Thirteen

Co-parenting and mental health

The relationship between co-parenting and mental health is complex. This theme examines an aspect of intimate partner support, the ability of the relationship between parents to provide support for maternal mental health and parenting within the family.

Jinny relates her experience of receiving support from a peri-natal mental health nurse who helped her and her partner to work together to support her mental health and take care of their children-

> *I had a peri-natal mental health nurse that came out to see me at home and she was amazing and yes helped me through going on the anti-depressants, coping strategies, what we could do, because I can always tell when I'm coming up to being quite.... I'm not feeling myself, so together with (partner) and myself we came up with ideas of what I could do to manage these before I had that blip and went into hiding* (Jinny).

The phrase "I'm not feeling myself" becomes a key word for them as a couple, that her partner is able then to respond to with coping actions-

> *So I noticed straight away quite soon that I'm not feeling myself, so I tell (partner) that I'm not feeling 'myself' that's the key word, and we change something within our day, so we don't stick to the routine we do something that's completely non routine for us* (Jinny).

The ability of Jinny to be self-aware to this level and of her partner to listen is significant here, both elements being required for successful coping to be implemented. The acceptance by Jinny's partner of his ability to have a role in the implementation of coping in this respect is key-

> *If I say I'm not feeling myself I just need a little bit of time to myself, because we've got very busy lifestyles, he will quickly grab the kids and whisk them off to go and see their grandparents or go down the beach or something just so I can go and have a bath, and just half an hour to myself* (Jinny).

The two main coping strategies that they then put into play are 'doing something different' and or facilitating 'time for self' for Jinny. Both are restorative for Jinny and prevent further spiralling into mental suffering for her. The value of this support for her as a person is significant. The making of space for her to have 'time for self' allows her to cope by emotionally down regulating and therefore be able to be more present emotionally for her children. This is a protective action by both parents for their children and minimises suffering in the family.

Isla talks about her husband's checking-in behaviour with her-

I think he was quite conscious of talking to me, making sure that you know he was asking me how I was feeling, asking if there was anything that I needed (Isla).

Isla finds this supportive; her needs are being thought about. She is aware that her feelings are being consciously considered and, in this way, valued. It is a recognition of her personhood.

Lynne expresses the difficulty faced by her and her husband when their children were very young and had additional health care needs, which needed very high levels of care-

> *My husband um we kind of hit rock-bottom really when (child named) was about a year old because he was sleeping on my daughters floor for a year because of how (second child) was sleeping and he needed to go to work the next day so even that relationship, you know we just didn't know who each other were anymore because we were just like ships that passed in the night* (Lynne).

The demands of work and childcare take a toll upon their relationship, but what is also evident is the commitment that they are both displaying to the care of their children. Lynne describes the recognition of the support that they both need at different times-

> *We've really had to work on that, that communication between the two of us, that understanding that we are both feeling certain ways at certain times, and supporting each other with that, but you know I've become a lot more assertive in saying... well actually no I need to do this for me.... or.... no you need to have her so I can go and just go and have a bath or something.... Because it.... not because he wouldn't do that it just doesn't come naturally to think....oh well I'll offer to do that.... if that makes sense* (Lynne).

Part of Lynne's coping has been directed towards improving her own communication skills with her husband; the ability to be specific in the communication of her needs and not interpret the lack of a particular supportive action in a negative way. This is problem solving in approach with adjusting of her actions to be effective. Lynne is able to recognise that her husband is not able to carry out specific tasks that would be helpful to her without her specifically requesting them. This is important to the success of their partnership and to the joint care of their children. It is effective in removing areas of potential friction and improving clarity within their relationship.

Kelly reflects how her husband struggled in his transition to fatherhood with their first child, but by their second child he found his role much more naturally-

> *My husband really struggled first time around, I think it was a big shock to the system him becoming a dad, but then this time around its all seemed kind of natural to him and he's been really good with my older son* (Kelly).

This acceptance by Kelly of her partner's lack of experience appears non-judgmental and positive in its focus on the development of him into being a father to their children. The transitions for mothers and fathers are uniquely individual and Kelly's ability to understand this process for her husband demonstrates adaptability in its coping style. The ability to be sensitive to each other's mental states and well-being is bi-directional and Lynne here also acknowledges that her husband has had time when he has felt low when one of their children was unwell-

> *You know he had similar like err down, low times when we were going through what we went through* (Lynne).

This acknowledgement is helpful in several ways. Lynne is not alone in feeling low. Understanding each other's mental state facilitates tolerance, and recognition enables coping actions to be taken at specific times when the person is feeling vulnerable.

Beth is also reflective about the needs of her husband and her responsibility to help him within their relationship-

> *There's the extra pressure on the man as well in the relationship, if the man's around, you know because you have a commitment to your marriage and um they are changing as well, but you have to help them through it as well, as a wife now, you know.... but, I don't know.... it's really difficult when you have got a baby that won't stop crying (laughs)* (Beth).

Beth is aware of the extra pressure on her husband as he is adapting to being a father and part of a new family, coping with things unknown. Beth's dialogue becomes disjointed as she struggles to be clear in her thinking, she ends up laughing as in apparent resignation and acknowledgement of how hard it is for her to meet his needs whilst caring for a crying baby. However, there is a sense of their joint struggle, something that they are going through together. It is difficult and transforming at the same time.

Grace describes how her husband is able to pick up on the warning signs that she is in need of a break-

> *Sometimes I think he's better than me at seeing when I need a break even because.... it happened on Saturday.... I think maybe I shouted at (second child) or something and I think it was about something... do you know something not worth shouting about and he was like 'Right so after we have breakfast, I am just going to go take them to the park and you can....'* (Grace).

The knowing of a person's normal enables the picking up of stress cues that can be helpful as Grace says her husband was aware before she was that she needed a break. Grace's husband takes supportive action which appears to be coping-based and is protective for Grace's ability to manage her equilibrium. This ability to parent in partnership is effective in promoting coping abilities within the family unit and for the benefit of the family unit.

However, Ava here talks of a time when her husband was 'taking' the baby to give her a break, but she was struggling with ambivalent feelings about this-

> *I just felt like he was taking him away from me, but he wasn't he was doing a really good thing, that I could get to bed, have some rest, feel a bit fresher for when they got back, tidy the house up, have a bath, whatever I needed to do, he was allowing me to do that. I just didn't see it like that* (Ava).

Ava's partner was doing the right thing to support her mentally and physically, but her anxiety and sense of loss at having to spend time away from her baby was making it counterproductive in terms of support. The balance and sensitivity required in co-parenting is challenging, even when both partners have the best of intentions. The early emotional bonds between Ava and her baby made it hard for her to be separated from her baby. Ava and her partner had to reach some sort of compromise that enabled her to rest, whilst not causing her emotional distress.

Chloe describes feeling disconnected with her husband in their day-to-day experiences of being a parent as he is out working and she is at home with the children-

My husband although he was a very supportive person he doesn't know…. we live in very different worlds, he goes to work and hasn't ever spent a long time at home with the children …

He's got to try to understand what it's like to be a mum, 24/7 and also understand the mental health side of things, whereas I've got friends who understand at least the 'being mum' anyway so it makes it easier for them to kind of wrap their head around my entire situation (Chloe).

The two things for Chloe, the 24/7 parenting and her mental ill-health, are unrelated experiences that make it more difficult for her to feel that her husband is able to understand her situation. However, she realises that when she is able to express how she if feeling it can result in her getting the support that she needs-

Some days, telling somebody else how I am feeling, is a really really vital tool, even if it doesn't change how I am feeling, it means that that person is able to understand me a little bit better if I'm going to come into contact with them, um and kind of often leads to more of the care that I might need, so if my husband knows if I am feeling like that he might come home (Chloe).

When Chloe tells her husband how she is feeling, she is enabling him to support her mental health and her parenting.

For Dawn looking back, she feels that she should have been stronger in asking her husband for help-

I should have…. have insisted that my husband helped and if he wasn't going to then I needed to know, am I doing this on my own or if you're not helping, we are not doing this as a team we need to…. just stand your ground, look after yourself (Dawn).

Dawn would like to feel that they are able to parent as a team. She identifies her difficulties in ensuring she has the appropriate support from her husband, as a lack of care for herself. There is an absolute sense of her struggle here and to know that she needed to do it alone would have been better than parenting in isolation as part of a couple. If she was sure that she needed to parent alone, she implies that she could have started to make provision for it. In terms of coping, she is reaching a point of identifying her limits. This low point of recognition that things have to be different is her potential turning point where she can start to prioritise her own needs.

Ellie talks about how her husband helped her adapt to being a mum and, in this way, supported her mental health-

> *My husband, I remember with (child) it was always 'I can't do it, I can't do it' but he kept going 'you've just done it' and that really helped* (Ellie).

His matter of fact positivity about her abilities gives a sense of calm, engendering confidence in her own abilities.

The relationship between parents can provide a source of intimate support that is pivotal to coping with maternal mental ill-health and motherhood within the family structure. The mothers' accounts give examples of bi-directional effective and ineffective support between parents. The subtlety that differentiates the two, evidences the challenges of co-parenting and mental ill-health, with effective communication being recognisably important for success. It is a learning experience for both parents as the double challenges of mental ill-health and parenthood together can be substantial. The roles of partners can be complex and influential. Partner support has been shown to take precedence over support from other existing relationships in terms of psychological well-being and life satisfaction and can be preventative in terms of avoidance of maternal anxiety and depression after childbirth (Beard, 2019). Having a partner who can understand and appreciate what is happening for you on a day-to-day basis is supportive for the mothers.

Co-operative parenting has also been shown to have positive outcomes for children and can impact the relationship between mother and child (Beard, 2019). The protective aspect of co-parenting and mental health is significant: the partner who can check in; the partner who can see the need for support even before a mother sees it herself; the partner who can support the day's coping by helping change something for the better. The mothers perceive the importance of bi-directional communication and show understanding that the fathers also need support in their new role as a parent. Crittenden (2008) points out that yesterday's children become today's mothers and fathers. What she means is that we all carry a prototype of child and parent into the role. It is complex and difficult and in the presence of trauma, we will all need support.

In the final theme we return to the mothers themselves as coping within the nature of the mother-child relationship is examined further. Mothers and children can be seen to cope together, inspiring each other and nurturing each other's needs within the dyad.

Chapter Fourteen

Mothers and children coping together

A baby arrives into the world, ready to relate with responsive caregivers, and is able to initiate interactions. In this chapter, coping within the nature of the mother-child relationship is examined. Stadlen (2004, p.95) reminds us that "each relationship is an original creation", we do not experience and cope with stress in isolation from others, but usually within the context of relationships. In this way mothers and infants can be viewed as a coping dyad.

To know who we are, we need another person who can see us. Or to put it another way, to have a "sense of identity requires the existence of another by whom one is known" (Laing 1960,1990, p. 139). It is understood that the factors which promote resilience are laid down in childhood and can be protective into adulthood, promoting psychological and physical well-being (Maselko et al., 2011). Our early attachment relationships equip us for the world we live in.

Schore (2019) describes the child's first relationship with the mother as a template, which shapes our capacity to enter into later emotional relationships. The non-verbal communications between a mother and baby often happen beneath conscious awareness but work to regulate the infant's developing central and autonomic nervous systems and body based emotional states (Schore, 2019). The baby relies on the mother for reflective responses to develop and maintain a lively sense of self.

The mutual love between mother and child creates a strong motivating force, creating a sense of meaning, identity and shared values which clearly influence coping attempts in new mothers. For the mother, a recognition of being part of something larger than the self can be motivating and empowering. Berastegui & Pitallas (2021) explain that resilience in the maternal/infant dyad attachment relationship is demonstrated in the ability to establish connection after disconnection. It is a mechanism of responsiveness and mutual regulation. As this mutual regulation occurs, it becomes a source of support for both mother and infant. This can enable the building of connections, competence, communication skills, and trust in knowing that we are understandable to others.

The desire of new mothers to give the best care possible is found in studies such as Dalby, Calais and Berg (2011), but feels however somewhat taken for granted. The hormonal systems that support our endocrine systems to manage stress and which motivate maternal caring behaviour are complex and intricate. Swain and Kim (2011) examined the 'baby-cry' responses of mothers and found that typically mothers find themselves highly motivated to care for their infants needs and experience interaction with their infants as rewarding. The hormonal shifts that occur when a baby cries, triggers the release of hormones including dopamine, endogenous opioids, oxytocin and cortisol, which act to promote parental caring behaviours.

The hormone oxytocin appears to increase the links between social memories, rewards and decreased anxiety when the baby stops crying. The mother and infant experience a happiness reward system that can motivate future behaviours. Someone to love, to care for, relate with, talk to, be loved by, to protect, can become a reason for coping, a reason for carrying on when things are difficult, a reason for living and can lead to an increase of empathy and caring feelings, enjoyment, purpose and fulfilment.

Ava specifically describes her child as her motivation to carry on when things are difficult for her-

> *That realisation of, that I've made this human, he's mine* (Ava).

The addition of routine, a need to meet with others, a feeling of social belonging, and the new status as a parent can also be supportive as Faye here describes-

> *I had a reason to get up every morning, I had a reason to live, I had…. you know, it…. like new life brings such joy, like to everyone and everybody wants to be your friend, you know, when you have a new baby, everybody wants to see you, everybody smiles at you in the street, it's just the whole world is a bit brighter I think when you have a baby* (Faye).

For Faye her baby gave her focus and direction, "it made me feel I had a purpose". This maternal/infant dyad can be viewed as the inner most layer of nested support.

In many ways the critical question could be 'what helps when this doesn't happen?' Are there still strengths in the mother/child dyad that can be tapped into? There is a hormonal role in co-regulation that is bi-directional, as with Faye who finds strength to feel that she can manage her situation in the moment after her child smiles at her. The serotonin love hormone stimulus is coming from her child to her and helping regulate her emotions just as her care to her child is regulating her child to feel safe, loved and cared for by her. This extract we heard earlier but is also relevant here-

> *(child named) is helping me although it is hard and you know like when she is really, really excited, to go to sleep and I'm stood there rocking her and thinking…. oh my gosh what am I going to do…. But then she'll turn around and smile and that's enough sometimes just to get through* (Faye).

The ability of coping to be both voluntary and involuntary is complex, with some strategies slipping back and fore between the two (Aldwin, 2011). When parents want to help their children cope in stressful situations it is going to be partly instinctual knowledge based on their own experiences of coping with adversity. Ava describes wanting things to be different for her child-

> *I mean as I've grown up I've always been quite stressed, quite anxious, and I don't want to pass that on I want to pass on a bit of calm and tranquillity almost of it* (Ava).

There is an instinctual protective stance that is an inspiration to cope and pass on coping strategies. The protective parental instincts are instrumental in the production of joint bi-directional learning, mother to child, child to mother. Learning to cope together as a dyad, positively influencing each member of the dyad.

Attachment resilience has been described as characterised by the rupture and repair experiences. Through these experiences of stress and restoration, positive coping learning experiences can occur that are supportive to both mother and infant. Coping changes from moment to moment, each hour or day bringing in differing aspects of coping as a phenomenon to bear. The nature of parenting involves a continuous changing landscape of events that require constant appraisal and re-appraisal: the baby is hungry, bored, tired, in need of changing, calm, upset, playful and so on. There is a flow capacity in coping with caring for an infant requiring a flexibility of response and attunement with the needs of the infant.

The mothers all give examples of pro-active, future orientated and protective coping towards their infants. Additionally, examples of empathetic responding can be considered a mode of relationship focused coping. Empathetic responding involves efforts to understand another person and provide support in a caring manner to defuse stress and maintain the relationship (Revenson & DeLongis, 2011). Infants need to be viewed as part of a relationship dyad with the mother. Tronick (2018) emphasises that the achievement of maternal-infant co-regulation is a co-creation by both participants. It is a result of the efforts of both mother and child together. In this way mothers and infants can be viewed as a bi-directional coping dyad who support each other in their coping efforts.

Motherhood itself can be a source of strength and the imperative to cope is high when looking after a vulnerable infant. Moreover, the development of a positive sense of identity beyond mental ill-health can be supported through motherhood as a source of identity and this can be an important component of personal recovery (Hine et al., 2018; Perera, Short & Fernbacher, 2014). It was at times easier for the mothers to talk about the ways of coping they wanted their children to have, than to talk about their own ways of coping. This advocacy role in motherhood is potentially strengthening for the mother and supporting their child's coping may reinforce their own coping awareness and understanding.

Chapter Fifteen

In conclusion

The mothers' interviews highlight the range and depth of coping resources that they use. There is no judgment of mal-adaptive coping here because it is important to recognise the role of mal-adaptive coping in our survival. When we accept our past mal-adaptive coping strategies, we can support the building of self-compassion which is essential to recovery. Our ability to be aware of our own coping strategies and those of other people can enable the building of resilience through building on effective strategies and minimising the use of ineffective strategies. This is aligned with the evolutionary concepts of survival.

The mothers in the study all describe placing their vulnerable infant's needs before their own. This altruistic stance appears to feel at times unacknowledged by the wider social structure of society. The ability to balance meeting the needs of their infants with meeting their own needs is critical to maintaining coping abilities and health. Some mothers related accounts of being at 'rock-bottom', feeling that their needs are placed at the 'bottom' of the pile, at the 'bottom' of the hierarchy of need. This can be a pivotal change point, but it can also be a point of vulnerability. The journeys that the mothers shared, show how they developed self-awareness, the courage to ask for help at often their most vulnerable, and their ongoing efforts to incorporate self-care into their lives. The mothers demonstrated a developing awareness and ability to acknowledge the need to balance the needs of the vulnerable infant with their own needs. There was an emerging significance for the mothers in being able to have a sense of their own mental health which was enabling to the process of taking back control. However, it is not easy for them and the balancing of needs is difficult to achieve and maintain.

Raising children may be considered the most important and complex task in our lives. Extreme cases of where things go wrong for parents and children are widely discussed in the mass media, but the vast majority of examples successful parenting are not so newsworthy, and it may be hard at times for parents to feel encouraged. The mothers in this study demonstrate the mental, physical and emotional effort that is placed upon caring for their children and the complexity of the coping relationship between mother and child.

The women in this study were brave and articulate in their willingness to explain the phenomenon of coping within their lived experiences of motherhood and mental health difficulties. Many of them expressed a desire to share their experiences specifically so that it might help other women in similar positions to themselves. It is with great gratitude that the researcher holds towards the women who participated in this study and hope that their stories have been respectfully and honourably treated.

Appendices

Research questions

The main research question for this study was:

What can women's lives tell us about surviving adversity and developing coping mechanisms, with particular reference to mental illness and being a mother?

The sub-questions were developed around exploring how mothers with mental health conditions experience coping-

- ❖ What are the lived experiences of coping for mothers with mental health conditions?

- ❖ How are mother's experiences of coping affected by motherhood and mental illness?

- ❖ What ways of coping come out of past experiences of coping, where does strength come from?

- ❖ What supports coping for mothers with mental health conditions?

- ❖ What coping strategies do mothers with mental health conditions want to pass on to their children in terms of being strong and resilient?

Research methodology

The research approach used in this study was a qualitative approach called Interpretative Phenomenological Analysis (IPA), which involves the collection of participant's stories of their lived experiences. IPA has an intellectual history of phenomenology, hermeneutics and ideography. These philosophical foundations guide its use, creating a layered approach, the central focus of which is the detailed examination of the lived experiences of the persons under study (Kirn, Huff, Godwin, Ross, & Cass, 2019).

IPA research prioritises the participant's view, appraising the participant as the expert on their story and exploring the meaning making processes of individuals by examining the language and emotions surrounding the individual participant's experiences (Clifford, Craig, & McCourt, 2018). It is essentially a bottom-up approach, which explores the meaning of specific experiences to specific people (Clifford et al., 2018). Husserl one of the founders of phenomenological inquiry considered that the essential features of an experience could transcend the particular and illuminate the experience for others (Smith et al., 2022).

Heidegger, a student of Husserl, influenced the development of phenomenology by the development of the concept of a person 'being in' the world within their own context of time, relationships, location and engagement with the world (Smith et al., 2012). Each person's way of 'being in the world' having a uniqueness that is at the same time framed within the universal nature of human existence (Boden, Larkin, & Iyer, 2018). Heidegger (1953, 2010) explains the term 'phenomenon' as meaning "something that can be encountered" or in a direct translation from the Greek "to show itself" (p. 27).

The phenomenon of 'coping' can be viewed in this way as something that can be encountered and that shows itself through women's lives. This will enable analysis of the phenomenon within the complex, nested relational, social and political environments, effectively utilising Bronfenbrenner's (1979) model of social ecology. The ability to get beyond preconceptions requires an awareness of such influences of natural assumptions and expectations on perception (Rennie, 1999). Husserl (1931,2012) emphasises the importance of being aware of our unconscious 'judgments' and to put them out of action by bracketing them (p.58). He developed a method of phenomenology which requires the researcher to 'bracket' (as in mathematical equations), preconceptions and 'taken for granted attitudes', in order to focus on the participants intentionality (Smith et al., 2012). This concept was important as the study aimed to be non-judgmental and not to hold pre-conceptions about how women experience 'coping' in their lives. Husserl (1931,2012) discusses 'doubt' as an important tenet of the researcher's mindset, putting out of action our natural standpoint or views to open ourselves up as researchers to new possibilities of understanding (p.57).

The second major theoretical concept in IPA is the hermeneutic theory of interpretation and the hermeneutic circle. Bowie (1998) describes Hermeneutics as the "art of Interpretation" which was founded by German theologian and philosopher Fredrich Schleiermacher, who saw it in terms of philosophical understandings of language and epistemology (the theory of knowledge) (p.vii).

Schleiermacher (1838,1998) himself describes the "art of understanding": there are general principles of understanding correctly what another person says and then presenting this correctly in a way that communicates this to another person (Schleiermacher, 1838,1998). Our ways of processing what happens in our lives are complex and dynamic, ever changing in the search for mutual meaning (Larkin, Shaw & Flowers, 2018).

The hermeneutic process encourages the researcher's attention and openness to the lived experiences of participants whilst engaging with the broader significance of the phenomenon being studied (Kirn et al., 2019). This concept prioritises our meaning making and focus on qualitative exploration of expression through language. Laverty (2003) cites Gadamer's (1960, 1998) understanding of hermeneutics as a co-creation that happens between the researcher and the participant, through a process of reading, reflexive writing and interpretation. This double hermeneutic, conceptualizes the meaning making of the participant, and also the meaning making of the researcher (Smith, 2018). The insights generated are a product of the relationship and interaction between the researcher and the data; this does not imply bias but accepts that knowledge is only possible through the interaction (Willig, 2013).

Lastly ideography is concerned with the detail and depth of the data analysis, how a particular experience is understood by particular people, within a particular context (Smith et al., 2012). The term comes from the Greek word *idios* meaning "one's own, personal, individual" (Greek-English Dictionary of the New Testament, 1993, p.85). The meaning in terms of phenomenology is not the scientific cause or effect, but rather its meaning in the way it makes sense to the individual (Svenaeus, 2010). The experiential phenomena of an event, process or relationship, for example, focuses on the individual's unique perspective and allows the researcher to concentrate on single case analysis or small numbers of participants within research (Bryman, 2012; Smith et al., 2012).

Smith (2018) describes the experience of the participant who reflecting on what has happened, attempts to make sense of its meaning leading to thought processes that are emotionally laden. The use of participant quotes in the presentation of results can demonstrate the ideographic analysis of data; it is important that the quotes are meaningful and accurately represent the participant's experiences (Farr & Nizza, 2018). Smith (2018) describes three levels of meaning: a literal linguistic meaning; the actual meaning within its own context; and the experiential meaning, in terms of identity, purpose or significance. It is this third level, which is in nature existential that Smith (2018) argues is the core of IPA: this experiential level involves building on the other pragmatic levels of meaning to achieve understandings of experiential significance.

Feminist research philosophy

The study also considered a feminist research approach. Feminist research is an interdisciplinary area of study which can be included in a variety of theoretical frameworks, but specifically advocates the value of reflexivity and power sharing in research practice (Leavy & Harris, 2019). Reflexivity can address how power comes to bear on the research process and reminds the researcher to be mindful of any imbalances, focusing an importance on the way we discover something and not just the content of the data, therefore prioritising ethical considerations (Leavy & Harris, 2019). Clifford et al. (2018) describe the feminist perspective as one which incorporates a recognition of diversity and focuses on empowerment of women.

It was the intention that this perspective would help guide the development of this research study that is with women, by bringing these challenges into focus and prioritising their consideration. By the linking of the research with the wider literature on what it is like to be a mother and women's experiences of mothering and mental ill-health, it was hoped to provide an environmental perspective within the literature that is listening to women's experiences. By using a feminist lens we can celebrate unique contributions from women, about women, that can potentially benefit women and parents as a whole.

Health and illness is a place in which feminist research philosophy has a role, challenging the construction of women as passive participants in research (McNeil & Roberts, 2013). Developing insights from the study of people's experiences has become a foundation epistemology for research into specific gender studies, especially those of marginalised groups (Cerwonka, 2013). There is an imperative not to do "violence to another" especially marginalised groups by speaking for them (Cerwonka, 2013, p.64). Part of this do no harm principle was the incorporation of a salutogenic perspective. Aaron Antonovsky (1996) presented the theory that the way people view their life can have a positive influence on their health.

The fit with IPA methodology is demonstrated in the use of verbatim quotes from participants that aim to truthfully represent and honour their contributions to knowledge formation and do not reduce individual participant's experience to perspective only. It can also be understood within the context of IPA, as a co-production of knowledge or as part of the shared horizons in hermeneutic interpretation (Clark, 2008).

Introducing a theoretical framework

Skinner and Zimmer-Gembeck (2011) hierarchical model of adaptive processes and families of coping was used as a theoretical framework in the initial analysis phase of all the interviews, to identify the ways of coping used by the mothers (see Table below). A theoretical framework can provide evidence of a researchers understanding checking and provides transparency with regards to the orientation of the study. The theoretical framework in addition to the researcher's experiential background and wider knowledge of the literature together, form the conceptual framework for the research. The model was found to be supportive to the researcher's ability to analyse the data by keeping the focus on coping as a phenomenon but was not exclusive from other sources of understanding of coping as a phenomenon that were explored in the literature review for the study.

A hierarchical model of adaptive processes and families of coping. Skinner and Zimmer-Gembeck, 2011, p.41.

Adaptive process 1.
Co-ordinate actions and contingencies in the environment

Family of coping	1.Problem solving	2. Information seeking	3. Helplessness	4. Escape
Family function in adaptive process	Adjust actions to be effective	Find additional contingencies	Find limits of actions	Escape non-contingent environments
Ways of coping	Strategizing Instrumental action Planning Mastery	Reading Observation Asking others	Confusion Cognitive interference Cognitive exhaustion Passivity	Behavioural avoidance Mental withdrawal Flight Denial Wishful thinking

Adaptive process 2.
Co-ordinate reliance and social resources available

Family of coping	5. Self-reliance	6. Support-seeking	7. Delegation	8. Social isolation
Family function in adaptive process	Protect available Social resources	Use available Social resources	Find limits of resources	Withdraw from un-supportive contexts
Ways of coping	Emotional regulation Behavior regulation Emotional expression Emotion ap-proach	Contact-seeking Comfort-seeking Instrumental aid Social referencing	Maladaptive help-seeking Complaining Whining Self-pity	Social withdrawal Concealment Avoiding others Freeze

Adaptive process 3.
Co-ordinate preferences and available options

Family of coping	09.Accommodation	10. Negotiation	11. Submission	12. Opposition
Family function in adaptive process	Flexibly adjust preferences to options	Find new options	Give up preferences	Remove constraints
Ways of coping	Distraction Cognitive restructuring Minimisation Acceptance	Bargaining Persuasion Priority setting	Rumination Rigid perseverance Intrusive thoughts	Other-blame Projection Aggression Defiance

Summary of study findings

The findings of this study were able to give voice to women's lived experiences of coping with motherhood and mental health difficulties.

1. Coping was in many instances a very practical affair for the mothers, tending towards soft-organisational strategies with a sense of needing to achieve mastery and a sense of coherence in terms of 'my life is manageable'.

2. Mother's emotional coping strategies predominantly featured self-talk with the mothers using rationalising self-encouragement to support their emotions, "It's not going to be forever" (Beth). The mothers described aspects of emotional self- regulation such as "riding the wave" (Chloe), and "just walking away sometimes" (Beth). Other forms of emotional coping included support seeking; however, the vulnerability the mothers felt in seeking support was

poignant and can be considered critical for service planners to take into account.

3. There was an emerging significance for the mothers in being able to have a sense of their own mental health, when the mothers were able to recognise the significance of how they were feeling, they could move on to an acceptance which was enabling to the process of taking back control.

4. There was a strong theme of experiencing a journey in motherhood which contained elements of self-neglect, as the mothers prioritised their infant's needs above their own leading to feelings of being "bottom of the pile" (Dawn), to one of self-realisation that they were unable to function in a balanced way without the ability to meet some of their own basic needs.

5. For some mothers there was a feeling of the loss of self as they transitioned from pre-motherhood to the incorporation of children into concepts of self, with the additional complexity of mental ill-health which can also involve a loss of self in some respects, "I've lost who I was" (Dawn). However, motherhood could also transform identity in a positive way, creating a sense of meaning and connection, providing a healthy life focus and a sense of normality in everyday life, creating meaning outside of mental illness, "it made me feel I had a purpose" (Faye).

6. The mothers demonstrated protective instincts towards their children, which were partly based on their own experiences of adversity. They all demonstrated a desire to pass on 'coping' to their children. The range of coping skills and strategies that that the mothers tried to pass on was intrinsically linked to their own skills and abilities. The

coping skills and strategies that they themselves have found to be successful are the things that they felt confident to pass on.

7. The mothers were able to identify effective support that for them was inclusive of encouragement, thoughtfulness, checking in behaviours, feeling accepted and believed in, not feeling judged and a sense of holding of their difficult emotions. Practical support was valued and included things that supported day-to-day living, such as cooking, washing, shopping, cleaning and supporting parental sleep deprivation. The ability to seek support from intimate and wider sources creates the structure of nested support, which can provide a safety net in terms of effective support.

8. There is a bi-directional coping relationship between mother and child, which create a coping dyad. The literature suggests that mothers are typically highly motivated to care for their infants with hormonal factors at play. Maternal infant co-regulation is created by both participants of the dyad, infants also support their mothers coping with behaviours such as smiling "she'll turn around and smile and that's enough sometimes just to get through" (Faye). The mothers are also able to be inspired by their children's developing personalities, some mothers described finding the ability of their children to live in the moment, the ability to not hold on to sadness and be happy in the moment. The mothers demonstrate a joy and fascination in their children that is able to support their parenting.

9. When considering the phenomenon of coping, it is clear that lived experience of not coping is difficult and sorrowful "and I had a really bad day, everything just made me

cry" (Ava). Where as coping is a kinder more uplifting experience "I've achieved something and also I'm not overwhelmed, you know that's a big achievement (Faye). Having a sense of coherence seems integral to coping, my life is understandable, my life is meaningful, my life is manageable.

10. In terms of planning for health and social care practice, supporting coping skills by building on existing strengths makes sense. Recognising that individuals are unique and have potential for strength and competence can offer a self-compassionate stance that can take account of individual vulnerabilities and coping choices. Being aware of and caring towards the suffering of the self can support the use of more positive coping styles including emotion focused and problem focused coping, and an increase in coping self-efficacy.

Glossary

Acceptance A person's ability to assent to the reality of a situation without attempting to change it or protest it.

Accommodation A process of altering one's existing ideas about how the world operates in response to new information and experiences.

Adverse Childhood Experiences (ACEs) ACEs describe experiences occurring during childhood that directly harm a child or affect the environment in which they live.

Affect regulation A concept in psychiatry related to emotional regulation, which includes the performance a person is able to demonstrate regardless of mood or emotion.

Appraisal Within psychological theory appraisal of a situation causes emotional or affective responses that are the evaluative process that construe relational meaning.

Attachment A psychological, evolutionary and ethological theory concerning relationships between humans, particularly relating to an infant's need to develop a secure relationship with at least one primary care-giver for normal social and emotional development.

Attunement The quality of being in tune with something, particularly a person, within relationships and often applied to parents and children.

Avoidance A person's efforts to avoid dealing with something that is difficult or stressful for them.

Cognitive restructuring A form of thinking which can develop an alternative view or behaviour that reduces psychological distress.

Coping A complex psychological phenomenon defined as managing or dealing with something successfully.

Defense mechanisms An unconscious psychological operation that functions to protect a person from anxiety and internal conflict.

Denial The refusal to accept a reality.

Dyad A pair of individuals in an interpersonal situation, a group of two people, the smallest possible social group.

Dynamic Maturational Model (DMM) A biopsychosocial model informed by neurodevelopmental research which views attachment as a lifelong interpersonal strategy to respond to threat.

Ecological Systems Theory A framework conceptualized by Urie Bronfenbrenner (1917-2005) through which individual's relationships within communities and the wider society can be examined. The five nested levels of external influence include: microsystem; mesosystem; exosystem; macrosystem; and chronosystem.

Emotional regulation A process by which individuals influence consciously or unconsciously their felt emotions, when they have them, how they are experienced and how they are expressed.

Epistemology The philosophical study of the nature, origin and limits of human knowledge.

Equilibrium A state of physical, mental or emotional balance.

Hermeneutics The theory and practice of interpretation of language whether written or spoken.

Hierarchy of needs model A model conceptualized by Abraham Maslow (1908-1970) which places five tiers of needs within a pyramid: with physiological needs at the base; safety and security at the next level; followed by belonging and love; esteem and recognition of accomplishments; and at the very top self-actualization.

Ideography The ideographic approach is one which focuses on the study of the individual.

Interpretative Phenomenological Analysis (IPA) A qualitative research approach which examines how people make sense of their major life experiences.

Intrusive thoughts Thoughts that can be distressing, repetitive and unwanted.

Mastery A sense of having control over the forces that affect one's life.

Mentalization The ability to understand the mental state of the self or others.

Metacognition The ability to think about how one thinks, including the recognition of thought processes including discrepancies in thought processes which are able to increase self-control.

Mindfulness A state of being completely focused on the present moment.

Minimisation The ability to downplay the significance of an event or emotion.

Pandemic An epidemic of an infectious disease that has spread across a large region, multiple continents or worldwide.

Phenomenon Something that exists that can be observed to occur or exist.

Phenomenology The study of structures of consciousness experienced from the first person point of view.

Post partum depression A major depressive disorder with a peri-partum onset, shortly before, during or immediately after giving birth.

Priority setting The ability to evaluate what is important or less important at any given time.

Psychopathology Abnormal psychology, mental health disorder or maladaptive behaviour.

Reciprocity A social norm of responding in an equal way to a person, making mutually beneficial exchanges.

Reflective function The ability to permit integration around specific problems to be distilled and generalised so as to be applicable to other situations including some that have not yet been experienced.

Reflexivity The consideration of the specific ways that the researcher has influence in the study.

Resilience The ability to cope mentally or emotionally returning to pre-stress status in a timely manner, successfully adapting to difficult or challenging life experiences.

Salutogenesis A term coined by Aron Antonovsky (1923-1994) that focuses on the factors that support human health and well-being, rather than the factors that cause disease. The salutogenic model was concerned with the relationship between health, stress and coping.

Sense of coherence A coping capacity described by Aron Antonovsky (1923-1994) of how people to deal with everyday stressors consisting of three elements: understandability; manageability and meaningfulness.

Social referencing Evaluating one's own modes of thinking or behaviour by comparing them with those of other people.

Specialist Community Public Health Nursing (SCPHN-health visiting) A branch of community health practitioners known as health visitors who generally have responsibility towards infants up to the age of five years old and their families. They take over from the midwife's care of the infant and hand over to the school nurse when the child is five years old. They work closely with primary health care teams, social care and education.

Theoretical framework The provision of a particular perspective or lens through which a topic can be examined.

Trauma The encountering of experiences that violate a person's sense of safety, order, predictability and justness, to the extent that person is unable to integrate the experience and bear the reality, becoming instead overwhelmed.

Withdrawal Choosing to minimise contact with others as a self-protective strategy.

References

Ainsworth, M., Blehar, M., Waters, E., & Wall, S. (1978). *Patterns of attachment: A psychological study of the strange situation.* Hillsdale: Lawrence Erlbaum Associates.

Ainsworth, M. D., & Wittig, B. A. (1969). Attachment and exploratory behaviour of one-year-olds in a strange situation. In B. M. Foss (Ed.), *Determinants of infant behaviour, 4,* 113-136.

Aldwin, C. (2011). Stress and coping across the lifespan. In S. Folkman (Ed.) *The Oxford handbook of stress, health and coping* (pp.15-34). Oxford: Oxford University Press.

Allen, J.G. (2005). *Coping with trauma: A guide to self-understanding.* Washington: American Psychiatric Press, Inc.

American Psychiatric Association. (2013). *DSM-5 Diagnostic and statistical manual of mental disorders* (5th ed.). Washington: American Psychiatric Publishing.

Antonovsky, A. (1979). *Health, stress, and coping.* London: Jossey-Bass Publishers.

Aroosi, J. (2019). *The dialectical self: Kierkegaard, Marx and the making of the modern subject.* Philadelphia: University of Pennsylvania Press.

Asher, R. (2012). *Shattered: Modern motherhood and the illusion of equality.* London: Vintage.

Bardake, N. (2012). *Mindful birthing: Training the mind, body and heart for childbirth and beyond.* London: Bravo Limited.

Beard, E. (2019). What roles do male partners play in the mothering experience of women living with mental illness? A qualitative secondary analysis. *BMC Psychiatry, 19*(1), 229.

Berastegui, A., & Pitilas, C. (2021). What does it take for early relationships to remain secure in the face of adversity? Attachment as a unit of resilience. In M. Ungar (Ed.), *Multisystemic resilience* (pp. 271-290). Oxford: Oxford University Press.

Berthelot, N., Lemieux, R., Garon-Bissonnette, J., Lacharite, C., & Muzik, M. (2019). The protective role of mentalizing: Reflective functioning as a mediator between child maltreatment, psychopathology and parental attitude in expecting parents. *Child Abuse & Neglect, 95*, 104065.

Boden, Z., Larkin, M., & Iyer, M. (2018). Picturing ourselves in the world: Drawings, interpretative phenomenological analysis and the relational mapping interview. *Qualitative Research in Psychology*. Retrieved from https://doi.org/10.1080/14780887.2018.1540679

Bogels, S.M., Hellemans, J., Van Deursen, S., Romer, M., & Van der Meulen, R. (2014). Mindful parenting in mental health care: Effects on parental and child psychopathology, parental stress, parenting, co-parenting and marital functioning. *Mindfulness, 5*(5), 536-551.

Bowie, A. (Ed). (1998). Introduction. In F. Schleiermacher, *Hermeneutics and criticism: and other writings* (pp. vii-xl). Cambridge: Cambridge University Press.

Bowlby, J. (1971). *Attachment and loss Volume 1: Attachment.* London: Penguin Books.

Bowlby, J. (1973). *Attachment and loss Volume 2: Separation.* New York: Basic Books.

Bowlby, J. (1980). *Attachment and loss Volume 3: Loss, sadness and depression.* New York: Basic Books.

Bowlby, J. (1988). *A secure base: Clinical applications of attachment theory.* London: Routledge.

Bronfenbrenner, U. (1979). *The ecology of human development: Experiments by nature and design.* Cambridge, MA: Harvard University Press.

Bryman, A. (2012). *Social research methods* (4th ed.). Oxford: Oxford University Press.

Burgo, J. (2012). *Why do I do that: Psychological defense mechanisms and the hidden ways they shape our lives.* North Carolina: New Rise Press.

Callaghan, P. (2015). Mental health and well-being in the global context. In P. Callaghan & C. Gamble (Eds.), *Oxford handbook of mental health nursing* (2nd ed., pp.1-34). Oxford: Oxford University Press.

Carver, C.S., Scheier, M. F., & Weintraub, J. K. (1989). Assessing coping strategies: A theoretically based approach. *Journal of Personality and Social Psychology, 56,*(2) 267-283.

Cerwonka, A. (2013). What to make of identity and experience in twenty-first century feminist research. In R. Buikema, G., Griffin & N., Lykke (Eds.), *Theories and methodologies in Postgraduate feminist research: Researching differently* (pp. 60-73). New York: Routledge.

Chao, R.C. (2011). Managing stress and maintaining well-being: Social support, problem focused coping and avoidant coping. *Journal of Counseling and Development, 89*(3), 338-348.

Chentsova-Dutton, Y.E., & Vaughn, A. (2011). Let me tell you what to do: Cultural differences in advice giving. *Journal of Cross-Cultural Psychology, 43*(5), 687-703.

Clark, J. (2008). Philosophy, understanding and the consultation: A fusion of horizons. *British Journal of General Practice, 58*(546), 58-60.

Clifford, G., Craig, G., & McCourt, C. (2018). "Am iz Kwiin" (I'm his queen): Combining interpretative phenomenological analysis with a feminist approach to work with gems in a resource-constrained setting. *Qualitative Research in Psychology*. Retrieved from https://doi.org/10.1080/14780887.201 8.1543048

Coffey, M. (2003). Relapse prevention in psychosis. In B. Hannigan & M. Coffey (Eds.) *The handbook of community mental health nursing*. London: Routledge.

Cozolino, L. (2006). *The neuroscience of human relationships: Attachment and the developing brain.* London: W.W.Norton & Company.

Cozolino, L. (2017). *The neuroscience of psychotherapy: Healing the social brain* (3rd ed). London: W.W.Norton & Company.

Crittenden, P. (2008). *Raising Parents: Attachment, parenting and child safety.* London: Routledge.

De Beauvoir, S. (1949, 1997). *The second sex.* London: Penguin Random Ensor, R., & Hughes, C. (2008). Content or connectedness? Mother-child talk and early social understanding. *Child Development, 79*(1), 201-216.

Farr, J., & Nizza, I. (2018). Longitudinal interpretative Phenomenological Analysis (LIPA): A review of studies and methodological considerations. *Qualitative Research in Psychology*. Retrieved from https://doi.org/10.1080/14780887.201 8.1540677

Feeney, B.C., & Collins, N.L. (2014). A new look at social support: A theoretical perspective on thriving through relationships. *Personality and Social Psychology Review, 19*(2), 113-147.

Friedan, B. (1963,2010). *The feminine mystique.* London: Penguin Books.

Gadamer, H. (1960, 1998). *Truth and method.* New York: Continuum.

Germer, C.K., & Neff, K. (2015). Cultivating self-compassion in trauma survivors. In V.M. Follette, J. Briere, D. Rozelle, J.W. Hopper & D.I. Rome (Eds.), *Mindfulness-oriented interventions for trauma: Integrating contemplative practices* (pp. 43-58). New York: The Guilford Press.

Greer, G. (1970, 2012). *The female eunuch.* London: Harper Collins.

Heidegger, M. (1953, 2010). *Being and time.* New York: State University of New York Press.

Henshaw, C., Cox, J., & Barton, J. (2017). *Modern management of perinatal psychiatric disorders.* Cambridge: Cambridge University Press.

Herrman, H., Stewart, D.E., Diaz-Grandos, N., Berger, E.L., Jackson, B., & Yuen, T. (2011). What is resilience. *Canadian Journal of Psychiatry, 56*(5), 258-265. Hine, R.H., Maybery, D.J., & Goodyear, M.J. (2018). Identity in recovery for mothers with a mental illness; A literature review. *Psychiatric Rehabilitation Journal, 41*(1),16.

Husserl, E. (1931,2012). *Husserl: Ideas.* Oxon: Routledge.

Karraker, K.H., & Young, M. (2007). Night waking in 6-month-old infants and maternal depressive symptoms. *Journal of Applied developmental psychiatry, 28*(5-6), 493-498.

Karr-Morse, R., & Wiley, M.S. (1997). *Ghosts from the nursery: Tracing the roots of violence.* New York: The Atlantic Monthly Press.

Khalifeh, H., Murgatroyd, C., Freeman, M., Johnson, S., & Killaspy, H. (2009). Home treatment as an alternative to hospital admission for mothers in a mental health crisis: A Qualitative Study. *Psychiatric Services.ps.psychiatryonline.org, 60*(5), 634-639.

Kirn, A., Huff, J.L., Godwin, A., Ross, M., & Cass, C. (2019). Exploring tensions of using interpretative phenomenological analysis in a domain with conflicting cultural practices. *Qualitative Research in Psychology.* Retrieved from

Kurki, S. (2020). *You can't poor from an empty cup, take care of yourself first: Constructing the self in on-line self-care discourse.* Retrieved from http://urn.fi/ URN:NBN:fi:hulib-202010064218

Laing, R.D. (1960, 1990). *The divided self.* London: Penguin Books.

Lancy, E.K., Lewis Hall, M.E., Anderson, T.L., & Willingham, M.M. (2015). Becoming a mother: The influence of motherhood on women's identity development. *Identity, 15*(2), 126-145).

Larkin, M., Shaw, R., & Flowers, P. (2018). *Multiperspectival designs and processes in interpretative phenomenological analysis research. Qualitative Research in Psychology.* Retrieved from DOI: 10.1080/14780887.2018.1540655

Laverty, S. (2003). Hermeneutic phenomenology and phenomenology: A comparison of historical and methodological considerations. *International Journal of Qualitative Methods 2*(3), 21-35.

Lazarus, R. S. (1966). *Psychological stress and the coping process.* New York: McGraw-Hill.

Lazarus, R.S. (1999). *Stress and emotion: A new synthesis.* London: Free Association Books.

Lazarus, R.S., & Folkman, S. (1984). *Stress, appraisal and coping.* New York: Springer Publishing Company.

Leadson, A., Field, F., Burstow, P., & Lucas, C. (2013). *The 1001 Critical Days: The importance of the conception to age two period: A cross party manifesto.* London: Department of Health and Social Care.

Leahy-Warren, P., McCarthy, G., & Corcoran, P. (2011). First time mothers: Social support, maternal self-efficacy and post-natal depression. *Journal of Clinical Nursing, 21*(3-4), 388-397.

Leavy, P., & Harris, A. (2019). *Contemporary feminist research from theory to practice.* London: The Guilford Press.

Levine, P.A., & Kline, M. (2007). *Trauma through a child's eyes: Infancy through adolescence.* Berkeley: North Atlantic Books.

Machi, S., Yamauchi, T., & Sugimori, H. (2016). Help seeking intentions for early signs of mental illness and their associated factors: Comparison across four kinds of health problems. *BMC public health, 16*(1), 301.

Manso-Cordoba, S., Pickering, S., Ortega, M.A., Asunsolo, A., & Romero, D. (2020). Factors related to seeking help for post-partum depression: A secondary analysis of New York City PRAMS data. *International Journal of Environmental Research and Public Health, 17*(24), 9328.

Maselko, J., Kubzansky, L., Lipsitt, L., & Buka, S.L. (2011). Mother's affection at 8 months predicts emotional distress in adulthood. *Epidemiol Community Health, 65*(7), 6221-625.

Maslow, A.H. (1954, 2011).*Toward a psychology of being.* Blacksburg, VA: Wilder Publications.

Maushart, S. (1999). *The mask of motherhood: How becoming a mother changes our lives and why we never talk about it.* New York: Penguin Books.

McNeil, M., & Roberts, C. (2013). Feminist science and technology studies. In R. Buikema, G. Griffin, & N. Lykke (Eds.), *Theories and methodologies in postgraduate feminist Research: Researching differently* (pp.29-42). New York: Routledge.

Monteiro, F., Fonseca, A., Pereira, M., Alves, S., & Canavarro, M.C. (2018). What protects at-risk post-partum women from developing depressive and anxiety symptoms? The role of acceptance-focused processes and self compassion. *Journal of Affective Disorders, 246,* 522-529.

Montgomery, P., Mossey, S. Bailey, P. & Forchuk, C. (2011). Mothers with serious mental illness: Their experience of "Hitting Bottom". *International Scholarly Research Network, ISRN Nursing, 2011,* 708318, 1-8. doi: 10.5402/2011/708318

Morris, A.S., Hays-Grudo, J., Kerr, K.L., & Beasley, L.O. (2021). The heart of the matter: Developing the whole child through community resources and caregiver relationships. *Development and Psychopathology, 33*(2), 533-544.

Neff, K.D. (2003). The development and validation of a scale to measure self-compassion. *Self and Identity, 2*(3), 223-250.

Oxford Essential English Dictionary. (2011). (Eds. Dooner, M., O'Neill, M., Allen, R., & Delahunty, A.) Oxford: Oxford University Press.

Payne, J., & Maguire, J. (2019). Pathophysiological mechanisms implicated in postpartum depression. *Frontiers in Neuroendocrinology, 52*, 165-180.

Perera, D.N., Short, L., & Fernbacher, S. (2014). There is a lot to it: Being a mother and living with a mental illness. *Advances in Mental Health, 12*(3), 167-181.

Peterson, C., & Moon C. H. (1999). Coping with catastrophes and catastrophizing. In C. R. Snyder (Ed.) *Coping: The psychology of what works* (pp.252-279). Oxford: Oxford University Press.

Rennie, D. (1999). Qualitative research: A matter of hermeneutics and the sociology of knowledge. In M. Kopala & L Suzuki (Eds.), *Using qualitative methods in psychology* (pp. 3-13). London: Sage.

Revenson, T.A., & DeLongis, A. (2011). Couples coping with chronic illness. In S. Folkman (Ed.), *The Oxford handbook of stress, health and coping* (pp.101-123). Oxford: Oxford University Press.

Reyes, A., & Constantino, R.E. (2016). Asian American women's resilience: An integrative review. *Asian Pacific Island Nursing Journal, 1*(3), 105-115.

Rothbaum, F., Weisz, J. R., & Snyder, S.S. (1982). Changing the world and changing the self: A two process model of perceived control. *Journal of Personality and Social Psychology, 42*, 5-37.

Rutter, M. (1999). Resilience concepts and findings: Implications for family therapy and systematic practice. *Journal of Family Therapy, 21*, 119-144.

Salovey, P., Bedell, B. T., Detweiler, J. B., & Mayer, J. D. (1999). Coping intelligently: Emotional intelligence and the coping process. In C. R. Snyder (Ed.) *Coping: The psychology of what works* (pp.141-165). Oxford: Oxford University Press.

Schaerer, M., Tost, L.P., Huang, L., Gino, F., & Larrick, R. (2018). Advice giving: A subtle pathway to power. *Personality and Social Psychology Bulletin, 44*(5), 746-761.

Schleiermacher, F. (1838, 1998). *Hermeneutics and criticism: and other writings.* Cambridge: Cambridge University Press.

Schore, A. (2003a). *Affect regulation and the repair of the self.* London: W.W. Norton & Company.

Schore, A. (2019). *Right brain psychotherapy.* London: W.W. Norton & Company.

Shor, R., Kalivatz, Z., Amir, Y., Aldor, R., & Lipot, M. (2015). Therapeutic facts in a group for parents with mental illness. *Community Mental Health Journal, 51,* 79-84.

Skinner, E.A., & Zimmer-Gembeck, M.J. (2011). Perceived control and the development of coping. In S. Folkman (Ed.) *The Oxford handbook of stress, health and coping* (pp.35-59). Oxford: Oxford University Press.

Smith, J.A., & Eatough, V. (2018). Looking forward: Conceptual and methodological developments in Interpretative Phenomenological Analysis: Introduction to the special issue. *Qualitative Research in Psychology.* Retrieved from https://doi.org/10.1080/14780887.2018.1540620

Smith, J.A., Flowers, P., & Larkin, M. (2012). *Interpretative Phenomenological Analysis: Theory, method and research* (2nd ed.). London: Sage.

Smith, J.A., Flowers, P., & Larkin, M. (2022). *Interpretative Phenomenological Analysis: Theory, method and research* . London: Sage.

Smith, R. (2010). Total parenting. *Educational Theory, 60*(3), 357-369.

Stadlen, N. (2004). *What mothers do: Especially when it looks like nothing.* London: Piatkus Books.

Strange, C., Bremner, A., Fisher, C., Howat, P., & Wood, L. (2015). Mother's group participation: Associations with social capital, social support and mental well-being. *Journal of Advanced Nursing, 72*(1), 85-98.

Stokes, B. (1981). Health. *Environment, science and policy for sustainable development, 23*(4), 42-44.

187

Stone, M., Kokanovic, R., & Broom, A. (2018). Care(less) encounters: Early maternal distress and the haunted clinic. *Subjectivity, 11,* 108-127.

Svenaeus, F. (2010). Illness as unhomelike being-in-the-world: Heidegger and the phenomenology of medicine. *Medicine Health Care and Philosophy, 14,* 333-343.

Swain, J.E. & Kim, S.S. Ho. (2011). Neuroendocrinology of parental response to Baby-cry. *Journal of Neuroendocrinology, 23(*11), 1036-1041.

Tronick, E. (2018). Emotions and emotional communication. In J. Raphael-Leff (Ed.), *Parent infant psychodynamica: Wild things, mirrors and ghosts* (pp.35-53). New York: Routledge).

Uchino, B.N., Bowen, K., Carlisle, M., & Birmingham, W. (2012). Psychological pathways linking social support to health outcomes: A visit with the "ghosts" of research past and present. *Social Science and Medicine, 74*(7), 949-957.

Vitaliano, P. Russo, J., Carr, J., Roland, D., Becker, M., & Becker, J. (1985). The ways of coping checklist: Revision and psychometric properties. *Multivariate Behavioural Research 20,* 3-26.

Viveiros, C. J., & Darling, E. K. (2018). Perceptions of barriers to accessing perinatal mental health care in midwifery: A scoping review. *Midwifery,*

Watson, D., David, J. P., & Suls, J. (1999). Personality, affectivity and coping: The dispositional basis of coping. In C. R. Snyder (Ed.) *Coping: The psychology of what works* (pp.119-141). Oxford: Oxford University Press.

Willig, C. (2013). *Introducing qualitative research in psychology* (3rd ed). Berkshire: Open University Press.

Wirz-Justice, A., Van der Hoofdakker, R. H. (1999). Sleep deprivation in depression: What do we know, where do we go? *Biological Psychiatry, 46(4),* 445-453.

Acknowledgements

I would like to thank primarily the mothers I have worked with and the mothers who have contributed to this book. They are our inspiration and our teachers when we aim to provide supportive services within health and social care. I hope that I have effectively listened to them. My supervisors for this research in Swansea University were Professor Amy Brown and Dr Julia Terry without whom I would not have been able to complete this research.

For my personal support I acknowledge my husband Steve for his patience with my long hours at the computer, my children for their encouragement and my friends for their enthusiastic interest. In particular Sheron Labouchere for her proof reading and grammar knowledge. Lastly, I need to thank my father for his support for my academic path. I had this opportunity and only through their support was able to take it.

Printed in Great Britain
by Amazon

53436304R00106